S0-BOH-068

# The school within us

SUNY Series, Democracy and Education
George H. Wood, editor

and

SUNY Series, Restructuring and Social Change
H. Dickson Corbett and Betty Lou Whitford, editors

# The School within Us

The creation of an innovative public school

## James Nehring

State University of New York Press

Published by
State University of New York Press

© 1998 State University of New York

For information, address the State University of New York Press,
State University Plaza, Albany, NY 12246

Marketing by Dana Yanulavich
Production by Bernadine Dawes

Library of Congress Cataloging-in-Publication Data

Nehring, James.
The school within us : the creation of an innovative public school
/ James Nehring.
p. cm. — (SUNY series, democracy and education) (SUNY
series, restructuring and school change)
Includes index.
ISBN 0-7914-3589-X (hardcover : alk. paper). — ISBN 0-7914-3590-3
(pbk. : alk. paper)
1. Bethlehem Central Lab School (Delmar, N.Y.) 2. High schools-
-New York (State)—Bethlehem—Case studies. 3. Educational
innovations—New York (State)—Bethlehem—Case studies. 4. School
management and organization—New York (State)—Bethlehem—Case
studies. 5. Laboratory schools—New York (State)—Bethlehem—Case
studies. I. Title. II. Series. III. Series: SUNY series,
restructuring and school change.
LD7501.D3746N44   1998
373.747'43—dc21                                            97-37704
                                                              CIP

1  2  3  4  5  6  7  8  9  10

For Jane,
Michele,
Sue,
Patty,
and Bill;
For Rebecca,
Abigail,
and Annalise;
and, most of all, for Laurie

# Contents

Good ideas for school reform are easy to come by. The greater challenge lies in translating good ideas into practice and getting them to stick. In the summer of 1988, a group of teachers in the Bethlehem Central School District (a suburb of Albany, New York) met to deliberate on a body of then-current school reform literature to see how it might relate to our students. We developed plenty of good ideas and dreamed wistfully of transforming our schools. That was the easy part. Since then, a number of us have attempted to implement just some of those ideas and we have found that the institutional barriers are enormous. We have also found that, having surmounted some of the impediments, the rewards of working with students and their parents in new ways is tremendously beneficial to all involved.

What follows is a narrative of our efforts to bring about substantial change in our school and community. It dwells as much on political and institutional issues (building support, raising funds, addressing the needs of various interest groups, recruiting students) as on the philosophical and curricular ideas we have put into practice. Above

1

all it is a story about six teachers and the courageous families who joined with us to create an innovative high school.

Many have described their school of the future, but few explain how we get from the schools we have to that visionary ideal. The process for reaching that ideal is crucial. Indeed, the ways in which we attend to institutional and political issues will determine the success or failure of any innovative project.

In the spring of 1988 a group of teachers in the Bethlehem Central School District requested that the District fund a summer committee to review literature on school reform and develop a kind of think-tank report. A number of us, at the High School particularly, felt restless with the system. We had been watching the nascent efforts of the Coalition of Essential Schools and found the commonsense  ideas at its core appealing: simplify schools, require students to clearly demonstrate their learning, place the teacher in the role of coach. We chafed against New York State's standardized testing regimen, the Regents Exams. I longed for a school with a strong sense of community where every student would be known well by the adults, where the kids felt as much of a stake in the ongoing life of the school as did the teachers.

The District funded our request, and we met for a week that summer to review the recent work of John Goodlad, Theodore Sizer, Ernest Boyer, Mortimer Adler, and others. The Bethlehem School system is generally regarded as excellent. The professional staff has built a reputation for quality instruction and programs that extends at least statewide. By all the usual measures of success, students perform very well. But deep in our hearts, those of us who joined the "Restructuring Committee" believed we could do much better. As part of our discussion that summer, we asked ourselves the question, What is it about my role that has led me to entertain the possibility of restructuring?

Following are the answers that each committee member gave. These testimonials speak powerfully to the frustrations and concerns felt by educators everywhere. They suggest strongly that the machine of public education, while not broken, may be running to design standards no longer relevant.

*I feel an ever building amount of frustration with my ability to interact with and therefore effectively teach my individual students. I have so many things in my mind I know I need to do with individual students, but over and over I ask myself, How? I see 127 kids every day—that's one and one-half minutes a day per student. In that time I must cover my content, which continues to expand, provide time to develop skills, coaching time to practice skills, and motivation time. Where is the time to develop relationships with my students or even to interact one to one with them? Where is the time to know them as people instead of a name with numbers after it? Their schedules and mine do not allow for that time. I want to be an outstanding teacher. I want to know I have influenced my students and have helped make time in school valuable. But I feel the frustration because within our present system that is nearly impossible.*

*—A middle school science teacher*

*As an educator, I embrace the principles of a reform movement aimed at narrowing the gap between what is and what could be—especially if it portends to allow us to more fully realize our capabilities as "shaper" of young minds. The energy that I derive from children and teachers coupled with promise will cut deeply into years of frustrations. I like to believe that I am a piece of the puzzle we call promise.*

*—An elementary school principal*

*Changes are constantly happening in education. A teacher must change direction often, according to needs of students, parents, administration, community. The system changes slowly, but the teacher needs to be flexible and able to change at a moment's notice. Frustration often is the result, as well as decreased morale and motivation. Often I have said, "Oh, well, I'll just go in my classroom, close the door, and be with my kids; that's the important thing anyway." For these reasons, I was interested in the concept of restructuring. As I sat on this committee, I grew in understanding of the whole picture, the concerns at every level of the system. Our concerns/problems were more similar than different. This gave me insight into possible resolutions that apply to all areas of education and have encouraging implications for the future.*

*—An elementary school teacher*

*I am concerned about how I'm asked to spend the math and reading money my classroom is allocated. I am also concerned about how much uninterrupted instructional time my students have each morning. If I am accountable for the quality of education in my classroom, I want more control over the purchase of first-grade instructional materials and the scheduling of my students' school day.*

*—An elementary school teacher*

*It is important to me to be able to participate to a greater degree in the decision-making processes that directly affect my student, my profession, and myself. To be valued as an individual and to be respected for my professional knowledge and experience is vital.*

*—A middle school social studies teacher and union leader*

*As a librarian, I have felt the frustration of working with my colleagues but feeling little collegiality. I feel committed to the goal of equal access to knowledge for all students, but I am frustrated by the constraints of planning time, student schedules, and the allocation of resources. This opportunity to explore ways to improve our school organization has proved to be professionally rewarding. I am excited about the prospects of "renewal" in our school through a process of "restructuring."*

*—A high school librarian*

*So much of my time as superintendent is spent in seeking compromise and accommodation. Instead, I want to join with teachers and ignite the fire of our idealism. Together, we can be better than we ever imagined.*

*—District superintendent*

*I willingly volunteered to be a member of this committee because it would allow me to better understand the process and possibly the benefits of "restructuring." My goal was to determine the possibilities for improving curriculum, teaching, and learning. There are many such possibilities, and I sincerely hope that we as professionals make every effort to work toward achieving them.*

*—District math supervisor*

*I feel fragmented trying to fill the role of administrator of a facility, teacher, resource person, advisor, and clerk. I feel the need for a balance to each day—a balance that will accommodate teaching classes, working individually with teachers and students, and maintaining the collection—the necessary adjustments of time, to administer a facility with its component parts. Restructuring the elementary school day, in my opinion, offers the most viable means of change outside the realm of budget considerations.*

*—An elementary school librarian*

*The role of assistant superintendent and supervisor is incorrectly perceived in the district. The common perception is that of bureaucratic authority, deciding upon and directing program initiatives, evaluation processes, organization of staff, etc. These roles would more effectively work as change agents, i.e., facilitators of change, a resource for problem solving, a coordinator of people and ideas to determine need and possible effectiveness, to implement or not, plans for implementation, etc. I would hope restructuring provides more opportunities to share ideas and responsibilities for program areas and, in this way, staff can operate within and see the district and its program in a more holistic way.*

*—District assistant superintendent*

*I wanted to join our summer discussion seminar on the restructuring of school to determine the implications for our middle school. Since then I have formed the opinion that our school in Bethlehem can become a better place for all of our children. I feel that we—as teachers, parents, and administrators—can work together in the decision-making process to make the teaching/learning environment in our schools more effective and more exciting for our students.*

*——Middle school principal*

We felt confident that the concerns identified here were broadly shared because they were in close agreement with numerous scholarly studies that were broadly based. Three recent studies, in particular, all empirically based and all nationwide in scope, brought out the same concerns that we felt most deeply: John Goodlad's *A Place Called School*, Ernest Boyer's *High School*, and Theodore Sizer's, *Horace's Compromise*. A fourth study, less empirical and more philosophical, impressed us also: Mortimer Adler's *Paideia Proposal*. Other studies and reports were useful too. Following are excerpted several of these which give a flavor for what the Committee read and underscore the close correlation between what we felt locally and what was emerging nationally.

Vast changes have swept over education in recent decades, and yet the structure of schools remains much the same. Over the years, a host of innovations have been introduced: open classrooms, modular scheduling, off-campus learning, to name a few. Some new programs were successful. Others were marred by poor planning or by excess. The basic pattern of public schools may make bureaucratic sense—but does it make educational sense? (Ernest Boyer, *High School*, Harper and Row, 1983, p. 230)

What we are proposing is not an effort to mend, repair, or polish up the structure now in place. What worked fifty years ago for a society with limited expectations no longer works today. Rather, we are sounding a call for a basic restructuring of our schools. ("Report on the Commissioner's Task Force on the Teaching Profession: A Blueprint for Teaching and Learning," New York State, 1988)

Basic schooling—the schooling compulsory for all—must do something other than prepare some young people for more schooling at advanced levels. It must prepare ALL of them for the continuation of learning in adult life. . . . The failure to serve all in this essential respect is one strike against schooling in its present deplorable condition. The reform we advocate seeks to remedy that condition. (Mortimer Adler et al. *The Paideia Proposal*, Macmillan, 1982)

As part of its finding "A Study of High Schools" identified five "imperatives" for better schools:

• Give room to teachers and students to work and learn in their own appropriate ways.

• Insist that student clearly exhibit mastery of their school work.

• Get the incentives right for students and teachers.

• Focus the students' work on the use of their minds.

• Keep the structure simple and flexible.

Simple though they may at first sound, these commitments, if addressed seriously, have significant consequences for many schools, affecting both their organization and the attitudes of those who work within them. (Theodore R. Sizer, "Coalition of Essential Schools, Prospectus 1984 to 1994," Education Department, Brown University)

Our Restructuring Committee produced a report that was distributed to all district staff members. The week of deliberations and the development of the report were stimulating exercises and there was some limited follow-up discussion around the district, but neither the report nor its discussion resulted in any changes in school practice. Nonetheless, a seed had been planted.

In the spring of 1989, a number of us decided to act, in a small way, to begin to change our practices. We developed a team-teaching pilot project that paired an English class with a social studies class in a double block of time. We hoped to give the students an interdisciplinary focus and allow for greater scheduling flexibility by the teachers involved. When the program was formally announced in June, some members of the faculty showed resistance. Why hadn't they been asked for their ideas? How would this affect class size for teachers not involved in the project? These were questions that made us pause and that were to influence our later undertakings. When we returned in September to begin the project and were given our class lists, we found that the paired classes were not perfectly paired. Some students were in one class but not the other. Attempts to remedy this inconsistency during the first two weeks of the school year caused only more irritation among the faculty, and we feared it might adversely affect the students. We scuttled the project.

After some months of reflection, I began to think that the problem with the team-teaching project was that it interfered with other people's programs. We needed an experiment that would be completely separated from the high school so that existing programs would not be threatened. In the fall of 1989 I went to the district superintendent with a proposal to look into the development of a laboratory high school—a kind of alternative school with an experimental focus open to all students and programmatically separate from the larger high school. The idea of a lab school harked back to John Dewey (there was a strong progressive impulse to our work), and it was reminiscent of the professional development "lab schools" connected with schools of education. An "alternative school" it was not, not in the sense of the alternative schools spawned in the late 1960s and sadly dismissed as too "radical" for the mainstream. Even while radical change is what we sought, we needed to be in the midst of the mainstream and could not afford to be dismissed because of popular misconceptions of what we would be about. The superintendent was interested but said he needed evidence of support before he could launch such a project. I decided then that I would approach the teachers' union with the idea. Union and faculty support was crucial, as I had learned from the failed team-teaching project.

I began to promote the idea at union meetings, conducted an informal interest survey among the high school faculty, and brought the results (which were favorable) back to the superintendent. The faculty interest was tempered by an important caveat. The faculty wanted to vote on the project before implementation. The administrative team and the school board did not give the idea of a faculty vote a warm reception, but the Board of Education approved it and we began work knowing that the union and the faculty were behind the project. It was now October 1990.

Next, we organized a design team of teachers and administrators. The team's immediate goal was to develop a grant proposal. This turned out to be an important exercise not only for raising some needed money, but also for clarifying our concept of the emerging "lab school." We wanted the school to (1) maintain an interdisciplinary focus; (2)  emphasize fewer topics of study in greater depth than the traditional program; (3) maintain a project orientation in which students would be mentored in self-designed courses of study; (4) actively build a community spirit with democratic governance; and (5) do all of this at existing per-pupil expenditures. Our grant proposal was ready in April 1991, and we began circulating it immediately to a limited number of foundations where we had some sort of entree. In June, the Klingenstein Fund in New York made a generous contribution. On the strength of that, the superintendent and I took the grant proposal door to door at area corporations and made a personal appeal.

Owens-Corning, Roure Corporation, and General Electric provided generous donations. We now had our funding. It was September 1991.

It was time to reassemble the design team, which we did with several new additions as we decided to recruit members of departments not already represented. We were eighteen in all and faced the daunting task of designing within a year's time a lab school that was both visionary and practical—all in addition to our regular responsibilities as teachers and school administrators. For a couple of weeks we fumbled around, not sure how to organize, but a plan emerged. We decided to divide the team into three small groups. The small groups were then given identical assignments: design a lab school with the guidelines outlined in the grant proposal by March of the following year. The grant money was used to pay teachers for released time from the classroom (five days each), planning sessions, and visits to exemplary schools. Our plan was to bring together the three groups with their completed designs in March for a series of intensive meetings from which we hoped a master design might emerge that would incorporate the best ideas from all three.

We hoped that by dividing into three smaller teams we could capitalize on everybody's best thinking. Also, from a logistical standpoint small groups are easier to coordinate than larger groups, especially in finding common dates for meetings. Finally, we hoped a spirit of friendly competition might push us to a higher level of excellence.

We went to work. The small groups began meeting, often at people's homes. An esprit de corps developed. Every other week the entire team would meet to update each other on progress in the small groups. We also set up several visits to exemplary schools around the Northeast. Typically, teams of three persons—one person from each small group—would go on a trip. We visited Thayer High School in Winchester, New Hampshire (then under the principalship of Dennis

Littky), the Scarsdale Alternative School in Scarsdale, New York (Tony Aranella), and Central Park East Secondary School in Manhattan (Deborah Meier). Also, one member of the design team who was touring in Germany visited the Holweide Gesamtschule in Cologne.

Halfway through this portion of our work, I became fearful that the small groups might become territorial about their designs and that, by March, it would be impossible to overcome their small-group loyalty in order to blend the three designs into one. Nothing about any of the personalities fed this concern, only a hunch that the dynamics of the process might cause such a problem. I mentioned this concern to the team, and we decided to hold the first of our intensive meetings in January to review, over the course of a half day, our work in progress. At this meeting I stressed that the work of the small groups should not be viewed as a competition where one design will win out over others, and everyone agreed that it should be seen as a collaborative effort. In that spirit we presented our work and encouraged all to freely raid ideas in other groups' designs that looked promising. This meeting also served to remind us of the impending March deadline and spurred us to get our work done.

Running simultaneous to the work of the design team were the efforts of another group. We had determined in the fall that community ideas and support would be essential to the project. We therefore established a community advisory group and invited our school's parent-teacher organization to select eight parents to join. We invited the student senate to do likewise with eight students, and a local banker agreed to serve as a representative of the town Chamber of Commerce. We held three dinner meetings with the Lab School Community Advisory Group during the winter months. We solicited their ideas for the lab school design and had them critique work in progress from the small groups.

By March, all three designs had been submitted. We gave ourselves a week before the first meeting to review each other's work. During this week, the designs were farmed out to colleagues not on the design team who offered for a small honorarium to critique our work. These critiques were circulated among design team members. We then held three half-day meetings to build the master design. We were able to obtain the services of Harold Williams of the nearby Rensselaerville Institute who served as facilitator of these meetings. His skillful guidance was essential in bringing us to consensus. We held the three meetings at five-day intervals to allow time for conversations and reflection between meetings. At the end of the third meeting we were largely in agreement on a master design. Then disaster struck.

The teachers' association and the district had been deadlocked in negotiations for a new contract to replace one that would expire in June. Impasse was declared, and the union asked its membership to withhold all voluntary services until a new agreement was reached. The Lab School faced a crisis. We could forsake the union and carry on, or risk the project and show solidarity with our colleagues. Conscience demanded that we do the latter. For two months, the project languished. Our not-quite-completed design lay on a shelf. The many complex conversations already in progress that were needed to bring the work to completion were left hanging. And our financial sponsors . . . What would they think?

Just before school ended in June, an agreement was reached, and suddenly we had a contract. It was time to go back to work, but we were all scattering for the summer. During July and August, several of us stuck around to carry on the essential conversations among design team, administration, and board. Through correspondence we were able to check the final recommendations with our far-flung design team. With cooperation by all, we were able to reach agreement on a blueprint to be presented to the faculty and board in September. Our sponsors provided no negative responses. In fact, one suggested it was wise that the design team had respected the bargaining process by suspending activity.

Briefly, the design consisted of a four-period day with ninety-minute periods. Rotating through this schedule were three interdisciplinary courses, each of which met three times weekly. Together, these courses (humanities, sciences, integrated arts) encompassed all the major disciplines taught in a comprehensive high school. In addition to these, students would conduct two projects, governed by a contract, each semester. Every Wednesday morning, there would be a special three-hour block set aside for a variety of activities such as field trips, student performances, guest lectures, and community service projects. The entire curriculum was to be guided by a schoolwide theme selected jointly by students and faculty each semester. All course work and projects would focus on the theme.

Shortly after returning to school, the just-completed blueprint was distributed to all faculty, members of the Board of Education, leaders in the teachers' association, and members of our community advisory group. We scheduled meetings with all parties to solicit questions and concerns and to consider possible changes in the document based on issues raised at these meetings. Members of the design team also agreed that each would present the blueprint to one of his or her classes to get a sample of student opinion. After this round of meetings, the design team held a work session to make final changes. In the course of these meetings, the board indicated its readiness to unanimously approve the program should the faculty vote go favorably.

At a regular faculty meeting in October 1992, the design team, along with the superintendent, board president, and teachers' association president presented the final blueprint. The faculty voted on the following day—75 percent voted in favor of the program.

After four years of dogged effort, however, the real work of school reform still remained ahead of us, for it lay not in writing, presenting, or conducting research, but in putting into practice the ideas that were dancing in our heads.

School reform projects vary depending on the setting and the personalities involved, so it is difficult and unwise to make generalizations from one experience. Nevertheless, some noteworthy factors played a role in the development of the Lab School up to this point.

First, the talent, energy, and devotion of the team. Staying with this project required persistent hard work for more than a year on something that seemed at the outset to have little chance of success. Despite the odds, however, the design team brought its full powers to the effort as demonstrated in the resulting blueprint. Teachers and school administrators are the chief resources in the national effort to reinvent our schools. To the extent that the lab school project came to fruition, it was because of people who became the leaders in its design.

Second, the faculty vote. The most potent factor in winning collegial support was the promise that no program would go forward without a majority vote by the school faculty. Any veteran teacher has seen many education fads come and go, each one touted as "The True Way," and for each, teachers have been prodded to accept innovations by school leaders who too quickly jumped on the band wagon. "Innovation" in the lexicon of teachers has unfortunately become synonymous with nuisance. The vote, however, put teachers firmly in control. The fact that teachers were leading the change, also, won the project favor in the eyes of many teachers. The vote also put pressure on the design team to include teachers in the process in every way possible. In short, the vote kept everyone honest. At the same time, the vote introduced an element of risk into the project. After all our work, the faculty could simply reject it and effectively end the project. The design document also stipulated a second faculty vote to take place three years after implementation of the program. This second vote would serve as a recommendation to the Board of Education regarding the continuance of the Lab School. While the second vote would not carry the decisive power of the first, it nonetheless was to have a similar effect of putting positive pressure on the Lab School teachers to keep in mind the concerns of faculty members not directly involved in the program

Third, administrative support. The Lab School was a risky venture from an administrative standpoint. It was highly visible and carried potential for controversy, it involved other people's money, it was subject to a faculty vote, it seemed to flout state regulations, and it challenged conventional attitudes about education. All of this behooved the innovators to provide evidence that it had a high probability of success. That the superintendent (Leslie G. Loomis) and the high school principal (Jon G. Hunter) supported and nurtured it was evidence of unusual courage.

Fourth, a knowledge base of professional experience. Our knowledge base in designing the Lab School was mainly the collective professional experience of design team members. We filtered everything we read, as well as all our observations at the schools we visited, through our own experience and judgment. The findings of published research were not the main determinant in rejecting or accepting ideas. For example, even though the literature suggested that heterogeneous grouping is superior to homogeneous grouping, our experience with kids in school said such was not always the case and, accordingly the design of the Lab School allowed for either arrangement under varied circumstances. This was as it should be. If a program is to succeed, the people who carry it out must believe in it. The best way to ensure that they believe in it is for them to design it themselves.

People who work directly with students generally have the best instinct for what works. The mind of the practitioner is a crucible of academic learning and practical experience. Given the opportunity to reflect on all they know and enact their vision of the good school (opportunities so often denied by the system), public school teachers and school administrators will do great things.

*Fifth*, visits to exemplary schools. Much more potent than academic research in honing our ideas, were the innovative practices of colleagues we observed in exemplary schools. The observations we made and the conversations we held at these schools presented us with new ideas and forced us to question our own thinking.

*Sixth*, the competitive/cooperative nature of our design process. By dividing the design team into three small groups, we created a situation in which everyone's ideas could come forward. It is much harder to hide in a small group of five or six than in a committee of eighteen. At the same time, the understanding that no one of the three designs would be declared the winner and that all would get equal credit for the outcome was essential in generating a positive dynamic.

*Seventh*, a hook to get the attention of outsiders. The fact that I was a published author at the time this project began influenced its development. This advantage was instrumental in getting the attention of school administrators, the community, and foundations. This same advantage, however, was a double-edged sword because authorship made my motives suspect in the eyes of some colleagues who perceived me as merely ambitious. It is important to remember that authorship is not the only possible attention getter, and every possible avenue should be explored.

Eighth, due attention to the ideal and the real. Many innovations in public schools flounder because they are either too idealistic or too pragmatic. Idealistic innovations may work in theory but have little concern for the setting in which they are intended to be implemented. Since a setting may include contentious personalities, labor/management issues, turf loyalty, and tradition-bound attitudes, innovations may never get started. Other ideas may be too pragmatic, designed to fit in smoothly within the existing array of personalities, professional roles, regulations, and traditions. They sometimes get adopted but eventually might run along the same tired tracks to the same tired destinations.

The Lab School design work tried to balance the ideal and the real. We kept our vision steadily before us and stretched to its limits the system's tolerance for change. Innovators will do well to ask continually two questions that run in opposite directions: Are we stretching the system far enough? and Can we make this happen in our setting?

Ninth, no gurus. The design team remained intellectually in charge of this project throughout. Our design was eclectic and was the product of our own reflection intended for our own school. We did not simply accept the program of any of the current education gurus because we feared that the demand for loyalty might supersede the need for a healthy skepticism and that matters of disagreement would be cast as issues of orthodoxy and heresy. We insisted on following our design because we recognized that schools and the people in them differ sufficiently from place to place such that no model, no program is suited to all. Nonetheless, we benefited from the work of the best scholars and activists (such as those already mentioned). Three of the four schools we visited belonged to the Coalition of Essential Schools, an organization that wisely recognizes the importance of local differences and the crucial necessity that teachers and communities lead change for their schools.

With a unanimous board vote and overwhelmingly favorable faculty vote behind us, our immediate challenge was student recruitment. Course selection takes place in January for the next school year. We had two and a half months to get the word out—persuasively. It is an easy decision for parents and students to support a new program in general, but it is much more difficult to commit oneself or one's child to a different and new (read unproven) kind of high school education. We needed to convince our clientele that the Lab School program was safe, yet different from the norm. We needed to promote yet avoid heady promises of student success that we could not fulfill. If the program was perceived as too far out, potential students would flee in droves. If we made it sound safe and "not all that different" from the conventional program, there would be no compelling reason for anyone to sign up. If we promised high student achievement and easy college admission, we would be setting ourselves up for disaster (first, because no matter how splendid the program, it is always possible some students will not succeed; second, because we would be establishing an expectation that the program, not the student, would be responsible for making success happen.) But if we displayed a lack of faith in the special merits of the Lab School, we might as well be sawing planks for the program's coffin.

In short, we were quickly realizing that winning the support of constituencies within the education establishment (teachers, administrators, union, Board of Education) was only half the race. We had trained for a long distance run and suddenly discovered this was a biathlon. We needed to convince ninety families in town that this was for them—by January. Some prudent voices were suggesting that we should delay a year, that there wasn't enough time, but we were tired of delay and feared losing momentum.

We devised a three-pronged campaign. First was the mailing in mid-December of a letter of invitation and a descriptive brochure to the parents of all students in grades nine through eleven. Second was an all-day series of informational meetings with students, held in place of English classes one day just before Christmas vacation. Third was an evening meeting for interested parents and students held several days later.

The brochure was glossy and good looking, designed by our district information officer. In hindsight, though, the text of the brochure (written by us) was too short on promotion and too long on humility. In an effort to not oversell the Lab School, we undersold it. For example, we pointed out that Lab School students would not follow a NYS Regents program and would not earn a Regents Diploma. This alone was enough to scare away people in a traditional community where a significant percentage of the work force is employed by the State Education Department. We also failed to adequately point out that in so doing, the Lab School offered a program that was not *less* demanding but one probably *more* demanding than the Regents program. Furthermore, we failed to adequately explain that our purpose was to break free of curricular constraints inherent to the Regents program so that we might engineer a bold new vision for education.

The home mailing included a reply card with which families could register their interest. We were heartened to see abut 150 cards returned in the weeks after the mailing went out. We thought wishfully that even though the reply card stated that no commitment was made by returning it, anyone who took that deliberate step was already a likely enrollee.

The in-school meetings with students took place several days later. We wanted to reach every potential student with a live presentation followed by a question-and-answer session. The only practical way to do this was to pull students out of one of their academic classes and hold forth in the high school's mini-auditorium (which seats about 250) all day long. I approached the English supervisor about pulling students from English class because I knew he and his department were genuinely supportive of the Lab School. They consented, and we made arrangements.

I did my shtick with overhead projector eight periods in a row to groups ranging in size from 50 to 240 depending on the number of English classes each period. The students seemed oddly uneasy. They were attentive but giddy, perhaps because they were unaccustomed to being consumers faced with a choice, unaccustomed also to a direct appeal to them (not their parents) to buy a different sort of product. The most frequently asked questions had to do with college admission, maintaining relationships with friends not in the Lab School, and access to special courses (advanced placement, specialized electives). The next day, Lab School was *the* topic of conversation around school. The mood of these conversations was sober. Students seemed to recognize the seriousness of the decision they were facing. Had the Lab School been immediately perceived as the "cool" school, I would have been concerned because it would suggest a cavalier attitude. Of equal concern would be a perception that the Lab School was a school for the gifted or at the other extreme, a remedial program for students at risk of failure. We'd felt strongly that the Lab School should represent a cross section of academic talent if it was to demonstrate a new approach that might be adopted elsewhere. At the end of the presentation we had the students fill out a short survey. Of some 800 students present, 237 indicated interest in enrolling in the Lab School. We were thrilled.

Two days later, everyone went home for Christmas vacation and, we hoped, households around town were enlivened during the week off from school with discussion of possible Lab School attendance. Apparently that was the case because our evening meeting for parents and students held three days after return from vacation was a grand success. We packed the small auditorium with close to three hundred people (mostly parents, some bold students). I ran the same presentation I had for the in-school sessions, then turned the meeting over to the audience for questions, which continued well into the evening. Les Loomis, Jon Hunter, and Judy Wooster (who had just joined the district as Assistant Superintendent), and I, took turns answering questions.

There was a mood of nervous excitement, excitement that the Lab School represented the cutting edge, attended by the sort of nervousness that one faces on the high diving board as you watch those ahead of you take the plunge, knowing that while you can still turn back, you've already mounted the ladder and await on the platform. Where the students had appeared awkward, inexperienced buyers in the education marketplace, the parents had an air of tough customers asking hard-nosed questions. Would their child get into college? Who were the teachers? By and large, they were looking for a sure thing. They wanted a guarantee that the Lab School would succeed for their child. They wanted the Lab School to fix their kids and get them into the college of their choice. Their questions placed us between the horns of a familiar dilemma—promoting the Lab School convincingly without making promises we couldn't keep. Les Loomis ultimately provided the best response when he pointed out that enrolling in the Lab School represents a risk but so does enrolling in the regular program, and that education is never a sure thing. After two hours of questions, the group slowly dwindled to a handful in the front, chatting with us. The mood overall had been extremely positive.

D-Day was Friday, January 14. That was the day students would make their preliminary course selections for the coming school year. During the morning announcements that week, I ran daily "infomercials" for the Lab School. The recordings I had prepared were botched the first couple of days so I got someone to cover my homeroom and I read them live. Something happened in the course of the week; the mood of the students toward the Lab School seemed to change slightly. The sober attitude turned somber, fearful as the moment of decision drew near. Perhaps my morning messages came across as pleading; perhaps it was the fact that some high school teachers were steering students away from the Lab School with negative remarks (disturbing but true), or maybe it was just cold feet. But something had clearly happened, as we were shortly to discover.

Occurring simultaneously with our promotional efforts was our hiring procedure. We had spent much time debating which should come first: teacher hiring or student recruitment. There were those that argued for hiring teachers last so that students would enroll on the strengths of the program and not on the personalities of the teachers. Others argued that given the small size of the program and the close student-teacher relationships implied, it would be imperative that potential students know who their teachers would be. One insightful colleague stated flatly that people don't sign up for programs, they sign up for teachers. As it turned out, I suspect there was much truth in that. In the end, student recruitment and teacher hiring occurred about the same time, not because of a conscious strategy but for the simple reason that we had much to do and little time in which to do it. Tangential to this is an interesting discussion I had had with a member of the design team about a year earlier, when we were first treating the issue. He, an administrator, argued for writing the curriculum, then hiring a group of teachers to implement it. I argued—unpersuasively—that to a great extent the curriculum is the teacher and that curriculum development at its best involves a personal reflective process by the teacher. It is idiosyncratic. The curriculum I design and implement myself will be very different from the curriculum I design and hand to another teacher to implement. As the Lab School has developed we have found teacher and curriculum to be inextricably combined. It is perhaps a basic fact that became only more apparent in a small school where personality plays such a large role.

In hiring teachers, we felt it was important to build in a team approach right from the start. Therefore, we devised a cascading system in which Jon Hunter and I would recommend the first two hires, who would upon their acceptance of the position join us in recommending the next two hires and so on. Though this arrangement was acceptable to all, there were a number of workplace issues that complicated the process. One issue was whether working in the Lab School represented an "assignment" or a "position." The former meant that technically it was something that a supervisor simply determined for a teacher. The latter meant that a teacher would have to apply, the position would have to be posted and advertised, and in general a more elaborate protocol would have to be followed. In the end, it wound up as an assignment, but we posted the opening nonetheless in all schools in the district since there was, after all, the possibility that a teacher in the middle school or one of the elementary schools might apply.

Another complication that arose as the result of this decision was that an extremely well qualified science candidate from the middle school did indeed apply. As pleased as we would have been to hire her, we really could not, since the teachers had to be drawn from existing staff. The only way we might have been able to do it would be if a high school science teacher was willing to transfer to the middle school or if a high school teacher quit or retired. About this time, the grapevine reported that a retirement was under consideration. Though I knew the teacher fairly well, I felt it would be unfair to approach him about the matter when clearly my motive was selfish. Others, however, must have made him aware of the situation because he approached me one day and very graciously offered that it was true and that the paperwork would be done in time to help us out. Through the interview process, Jane Feldmann, the middle school science teacher, became our clear choice. She and Michele Atallah, a superb second-language teacher at the high school and a member of the design team were our first two hires. The timing was such that we were able to announce the Lab School's first three teachers (including myself) at the evening meeting for parents.

It was as the three of us and Jon Hunter were beginning to consider the next two hires that the bottom fell out of the program. Two years earlier, when we were considering how large the program should be, we decided we ought to be flexible in order to accommodate whatever level of interest the community showed. Therefore, we determined that the Lab School could range anywhere from 92 to 120 students with anywhere from 6 to 7.8 teachers. The program could fly at any of those sizes. The student-teacher ratio was derived from the high school's existing ratio. We added up the number of teachers at the high school, subtracted those departments whose services the Lab School would not provide (special education, media center, guidance, part of music), then divided the total number of students in the high school by that number. The resulting ratio was 15.4 to 1.

Despite our effort to be flexible, we had not been flexible enough. On the Friday of preliminary course sign-ups, Michele Atallah and I tallied the Lab School total. The number was a very disappointing 61. Were four years of dogged effort about to go up in smoke? My immediate thought was that somehow the numbers had to be increased. If we could recruit about another twenty-five students in the coming week—before final course selections were made—it might put us close enough to our target of ninety-two. Surely there must be a couple dozen fence sitters out there.

Recruitment is a thorny concept in a public high school as it lays bare some unresolved issues within the system. Should teachers compete with one another for students? If teachers compete, what are the rules of the game? If teachers compete with one another, can they still work collaboratively as colleagues? If teachers are not to compete for students, then how does one promote a course or program? Because these issues are unresolved, the institution is generally wary of heavy promoting. At the same time, recent years in our school had seen promotional activity by teachers in some subjects that were experiencing low enrollments. Promotional efforts consisted largely of poster campaigns around school and word of mouth. While I wanted passionately for the Lab School to succeed, I did not want to overstep the bounds of what was acceptable in the way of promotion. First, I called some colleagues who were very supportive of the program and asked them to talk it up in the coming week. I asked the Guidance Department what they could do and, while they felt it would be wrong to steer particular students to the program, they assured me they would make every effort to ensure that all students were informed about it. I also asked for and was granted permission to station myself in the gymnasium with guidance counselors on the day of final course selection to be available to students.

In the end, none of this changed anything. When we counted the numbers the following Friday, we had sixty-one students, presumably the same sixty-one as the previous week. During the week leading up to this day I had been considering how we might go ahead with the program even if we did not get the anticipated numbers. To do so, two principles would have to be upheld. First, any modification would have to be in staffing only; we could not touch the program because if we did, we would be delivering to students something other than what we had advertised. Second, whatever changes we made in staffing would have to preserve the student-teacher ratio previously worked out. I spent hours looking over the schedule, considering possibilities, and in the course of the week lost five pounds. Our fledgling program teetered on the edge of the abyss. Working closely with the Lab School schedule, however, was instructive. We had not until then attempted to section out students and work out each teacher's weekly schedule. Now that I was doing it, a number of possibilities emerged. As I discussed it with the two other chief writers of the Lab School design document (social studies teacher Marsha Buanno and science teacher Roberta Rice) a best solution emerged. We would go with fifty-one students and 3.0 FTE (Full Time Equivalent) teachers. The students would include all sophomores and juniors who enrolled. The ten courageous seniors who had signed up would unfortunately have to be sent letters of regret. With the reduced staffing it would be impractical to expect the teachers to differentiate instruction across three grade levels.

Also, in spite of reduced staffing, we would still have to include teachers certified in English, social studies, math, science, and second language. The only way to accomplish this would be for each of the permanent teachers to teach part-time in the high school. Michele, Jane, and I would each teach two regular high school courses during periods three and four when the visiting teachers would be teaching the Lab School students. Thus, we could deliver the program to fewer students (the fifty-one sophomores and juniors who signed up) while holding fast to all our commitments: consistent student-teacher ratio, identical program, coverage of all subject areas.

We presented this to the administrative team on Friday afternoon when the final number came in at the end of January. It seemed do-able with one major caveat: the faculty would have to vote on it again. To some of the administrators, this seemed ridiculous, it was after all the same program, so why must there be a new vote? But to the teachers present, a vote seemed a definite requirement. Were there no vote, some teachers would certainly object, asserting, on questionable but arguable grounds, that this was not the program they had voted on in October. There was some indication too that the more committed anti-Lab School teachers might stage a public protest before the board. Eventually, the administrators saw the wisdom of a vote.

While the vote was necessary, I certainly did not look forward to it now that students had signed up for courses, teachers were being shuffled around, and new room assignments were being discussed, individual teachers might find it harder to be as generous toward the Lab School. Voting on the Lab School now might be analogous to a vote on the American Declaration of Independence in the dark days of 1777 as the bullets were flying and the excitement of the patriot cause had become less giddy.

We first held several formal sessions with the design team. There was fairly ready acceptance of the alternate plan. The greater challenge lay in winning a positive vote from the faculty. The biggest concern was how the Lab School would affect class size in the high school. The issue was no different from the one in November, only now we knew specifically which teachers were to be in the Lab School (Jane, Michele, myself, and an undetermined math teacher), and departments had begun early talk about who was going to teach what next year. It's fairly easy to vote for a new program knowing that it may involve a new course preparation or new room assignment for someone somewhere, but when you or your friend have been asked to teach a new course and your room of twenty-five years may be changed, it's different.

Jon Hunter agreed to turn over the larger portion of the next two faculty meetings to discussion of the Lab School. Once again, the design team assembled in the front of the room and we presented plan B. This time there were some tough critics in the audience: Can you guarantee that class size in the high school will not go up because of the Lab School? Can you assure us that no one's job or any portion of a job will be lost due to the Lab School? Given the enormous effort made by the Lab School teachers and the sacrifices to be made by the high school faculty, what added compensation will the Board of Education give to show support for this program? These were all reasonable questions pushed to polemics by circumstances. To the first question on class size we could offer a good degree of predictability that classes would not increase. Could we guarantee it? No. To the question of jobs, we repeated the language from the Design Document assuring job protection. But in this climate, even that was for some not enough. To the question of board support, we could only repeat that from the start, we had been committed to doing the program at cost. Again, under normal circumstances, such as prevailed during the October vote, these answers would have been sufficient; but under pressure, the faculty wanted oaths and iron-clad guarantees.

Through two faculty meetings and endless faculty room debate, we endured resolutely. The design team admirably hung on, held their temper, and on February 9, we voted.

The tally was 45 to 41 in favor of the Lab School. We'd done it. Barely. There was some scrutiny given to the vote by the opposition. One colleague challenged the right of building administrators to vote and forced me to produce documentation (previously voted on by union members) vouching for it. Another colleague told me in no uncertain terms that in the months ahead, if it came down to his program or the Lab School, his would come first. But there were others, a slim majority presumably, who shared our sense of victory over the odds, who offered congratulation and thanked us for hanging on.

The following week, mid-winter vacation, Laurie and I left for a long-anticipated vacation in Key West while my parents came into town to watch the kids.

There is an important footnote to this episode. During the very stressful days of January, when the Lab School wavered on the brink, Laurie was a great support. She compared the creation of the Lab School to childbirth with a story that might inspire anyone to overcome the odds.

"I remember," she said, "when I was giving birth to Abigail (our second child); I'd been pushing hard for quite a while. I was exhausted and she was only beginning to crown. The doctor said just one more push. So I pushed. I gave it everything I had, but she didn't come. On the next contraction when the doctor said push, again, I said, 'I can't.' I had no more strength. And everyone in the room chorused back, 'Yes, you can!' So I pushed. I don't know where the strength came from. I guess it came from all of you. And with that push, our daughter was born."

As with the design phase of the Lab School, this episode, too, is highly idiosyncratic. It is unlikely that the particular mix of circumstances and events that surrounded our work would repeat itself in any other similar project. Nonetheless, there are some generalizations that are likely to have broad applicability and might serve as recommendations to others who would endeavor any substantial school-reform project in a public system, whether a school within a school, a charter school, an alternative program of choice, or anything similar.

1. Show faith and optimism in promotion of your program while avoiding hype. Your clientele want to know first that *you* believe in your program. Make your own faith clear, but be wary of making promises you cannot keep. If your program is truly educational you cannot guarantee results. Education requires the collaboration of teacher, student, and family. Teachers alone can't make it work and to suggest that you can without the commitment of student and family is not only incorrect but establishes an expectation even before students are enrolled that the student's role and the parents' role are passive, that whatever the program will do, it will do *to* the child and *for* the family. If your goal is a dynamic collaboration of all parties, build that concept into the promotion. Whatever you do, do not allow families to establish unrealistic expectations. Disillusion them of their naive beliefs that school will do it all for them. Les Loomis's

remark that risk is a factor whether you place your child in a new and different program or a more conventional one is very apt. There is as much pedagogical wreckage strewn along the sides of conventional pathways as there is along the road to innovation.

2. Sell both program and staff. My colleague's remark that parents choose on the strengths of teachers and not on the strength of a program is true, but if your families choose your program because of a particular teacher and that teacher leaves, you're sunk. A balance needs to be struck. If you know who the teachers are, say so; but be quick to caution families against choosing solely because of a particular teacher. Usually, in a program of this kind, there is at least one personality associated with it—the person who has led its development and will lead its implementation. Therefore, even if teachers are not yet hired during the promotional period, there is still a personality attached to the program and hence someone in whom potential clients can determine whether they want to place their faith and trust.

3. Curriculum should be developed by the teachers who will teach it. The best teaching occurs when teachers are granted the time and opportunity to reflect on their own practice and develop curriculum out of their own experience and knowledge base. Conversely, some of the worst teaching occurs when teachers are handed a manual and instructed to follow it cookbook fashion. At the same time, however, the school will lose meaning and purpose if the curriculum becomes an educational free-for-all. There should be a clear mission statement to guide the school's work. And teachers should be selected based in part on the fact that they buy into the school's raison d'être . Beyond that, however, curriculum development is a dynamic process that emerges out of the interactions among involved persons under the leadership of the teachers. It cannot and should not be overly controlled by outside forces.

4. Be closely attuned to the local politics surrounding issues of student recruitment. Public education has for so long been run like a socialist state that any kind of marketing or promotion is not only alien but threatening because it suggests competition and winners and losers (not among the students but among the educators who compete for their business). While you may be tempted to say *to hell with all the old grumps who don't accept my great new program,* you will do well to keep your enemies as few in number as possible. Be sensitive to the norms of your local educational establishment. It is the compassionate thing to do and it is politically a prudent course to follow. In the case of the Lab School, this approach has been essential, since the program is literally embedded in a host school. But even in situations where the links to other schools are fewer and less immediate, it is better to build alliances than alienate colleagues. Since the development of a new school carries with it an implied criticism of the status quo, you create from the start a reason for educators to regard you as suspect—better to give them no further reason.

5. Be sensitive to the concerns of your students. Student opinion about your program is extremely important. Most parents will announce publicly that *they* make the decisions regarding their children's education but they will confess privately that it is ultimately up to the child. In hindsight, we did not pay enough attention to student opinion. Despite our community advisory group (which included students), our test run of the program in selected classes, and our direct promotional appeal in school, it wasn't enough. Find out early on what reservations students might have about your offering, then address them. In our case, students were concerned about being separated from their friends, being stigmatized by the rest of the school, a lack of specialized elective courses, and college admission (a concern they shared with their parents). Some concerns simply cannot be fully

allayed until the program has been operational for several years and has a proven track record. Others can be addressed, and should be addressed early and often.

6. Promote the whole educational package. In all likelihood, the program you are developing is small, at least smaller than the established program from which you are drawing your students. One of the reservations about joining the new program that students and parents will undoubtedly express is that the course offerings are more limited. They're right. Course offerings are limited. Therefore, you must speak forcefully to the point that abundant course offerings does not ensure a sound education. You need to stress that what matters is a child's total educational experience. Is it coordinated, does it follow a logical progression, does it make sense to the student? Do the teachers see enough of the student to really help her learn? The strengths of a small program lie in these areas, and they must be stressed in order to disabuse your clientele of the naive belief that lots of course offerings mean a sound education. Safer to assume that in most cases it implies the opposite, since the institution's energy is focused on developing courses and programs, not children.

7. Don't give up. At numerous junctures, the Lab School has faced an imminent demise, but we did not give up. Sometimes we felt we wanted to, but we hung on because we knew deep in our hearts that it was the right thing to do. Even if the Lab School were to crumble and fall, there would still be a desire to try again, somewhere, somehow. Schools must and will change. There are enough of us now who believe that passionately. You have many allies. The scales are tipping slowly, inexorably against the status quo.

# 3

An undertaking such as the Lab School may be likened to a cross-country meet with high hurdles. Such a thing does not exist as far as I know, but for school restructuring it is an apt comparison. The terrain is uneven and winding, each turn yields new surprises. There are always roots and rocks to stumble over and twist an ankle on. To make the course a greater challenge still, there are hurdles placed at blind turns. There is one forgiving element. Like hurdle events in track and field, one need not neatly clear every hurdle but merely make it past each in whatever manner. You can plow right through them, or kick them down, as long as you keep on going. So doing, however, slows you down and causes greater fatigue. The trick is knowing how to jump, how to land, and how, by whatever means, to keep on going.

The week that Laurie and I spent in Florida, at the most remote southerly point from Albany in the continental United States, was indeed welcome. I indulged a fantasy and walked one day to the Board of Education office on Key West and inquired about teaching positions that might become available for the coming school year. It seemed very possible, they told me, that there would be an English job or two. Armed with this knowledge, the latest Keys Real Estate Guide, and a listing of used sailboats for sale, from the marina near our hotel, I spent an afternoon plotting our new life. As long as I played it straight at school, did my standard teacher thing without making any waves, we could spend our holidays and summers sailing around the Caribbean and late afternoons lolling in the backyard pool. Laurie, however, injecting an element of realism, suggested that within two years I would launch some kind of school restructuring effort that would place me at the center of a political storm and the boat would collect barnacles while the pool grew algae. She was right.

The first order of business upon returning to school was to convene the group of colleagues that was to ascertain the impact of the Lab School on enrollments in other high School courses. The group (sanctioned by the original Lab School document) came to be known as the Impact Committee and true to the punctiliousness of our faculty, even the composition of this group was the subject of scrutiny and objection. Who should select the representatives? From which departments should they be drawn? Should they be strictly union reps? Should Nehring be part of it? These issues were ironed out—Nehring could participate but not as a voting member—and the group met to review enrollment figures for next year's courses. The overriding concern of the Impact Committee was that no teacher's position should be ill affected by the existence of the Lab School. Specifically, the committee was to certify that Lab School enrollments did not cause a decline in any high school course that would result in the course being dropped for low enrollments. Nor should any high school class enrollment be driven up to an onerous level as a result of the Lab School. How all this was to be tracked, I don't think anybody really knew, but the Impact Committee met, scrutinized numbers, made all the numbers available to the faculty at large, and was ultimately, apparently satisfied. Not completely satisfied myself by mere numbers on a chart, I went to several teachers whose classes seemed most vulnerable and asked if they felt the Lab School had caused a decline in their programs. They said no.

Politics has always threatened to overwhelm the Lab School. Consequently, it has taken discipline and concentration to address the curricular issues instead of whatever imposing political storm seemed more urgent at the moment. As the starting date of the Lab School loomed, we felt under increasing pressure to get our act together. Michele, Jane, and I requested time off to develop curriculum. The district granted us the equivalent of one day every two weeks (substitutes would cover our classes) until the end of the school year. We met for the first time in March, and though we had a full agenda, we spent probably the first two hours commenting on the list of students who signed up. My guess is that most curriculum "experts" would not have sanctioned the discussion as we traded insights about this boy and that girl. But most "experts" are not high school teachers and do not feel the compelling need to know something—anything—about their students. Even if that knowledge is not borne out by one's further experience with the student, it is a psychological starting point—to be proven either right or wrong, but in either case a help, a crude chart with which to navigate and which admittedly will be altered many times. Thus we frittered away a morning with this casual—and oh so important—discussion.

Then we talked about exit outcomes, though we did not use that phrase. In the course of the Lab School's development, I have adopted a procedural rule: abandon a term as soon as it becomes trendy. There are three axioms behind this. The first is tactical. Whatever is "in" will eventually be out. And the more "in" it is, the further "out" it will become. If a program is to outlive trends and fads it must transcend them. The second reason is semantic: the trendier the word, the fuzzier its meaning. As soon as something becomes popular, second-rate minds start to cash in on it and, like hack shops in the fashion world ironing popular designer labels on the same old cheap clothes, school people write the latest terms into the same old programs. Pretty soon the new concept—however worthy it may have originally been—loses all meaning. Third, most "new" ideas may be described in everyday language. Why create needlessly an entire new lexicon unless the intent is merely to befuddle.

Jargon aside, the thinking surrounding "exit outcomes" is tantalizing. It derived from a popular trend known as outcomes-based education, the essence of which is two simple ideas: that students should not graduate from school until they know their stuff, and that schools should be judged not by how they structure their programs but by the results they demonstrate in their graduates. The first ought to be a fundamental premise of education. That we have to invent a new term in order to assert its importance suggests how far we have strayed from sound practice. The second of these ideas is basic, too. It is that methods matter not; what counts is the result. No matter what the style of the coach, can the team play football? If the students can perform the task at the end, then grant the teacher license to use whatever means work, even if they are a little unorthodox.

This second one is a useful idea, but there are pitfalls to judging a school by its graduates. One is that a school that makes much progress with less able youngsters may be judged inferior to a program that does little to advance the skill of students who come to school already skilled and able. The other is more hidden. What if students have indeed learned much in school, but what they have learned is not apparent in any measure (tests, surveys, college admissions) that may be applied. Only years later, perhaps, does that learning manifest itself in useful ways. If a school, say, asserts that it teaches honesty and democratic values and the teachers assert that indeed the school does this, but there is no clear measure that upon graduation students are more honest and more democratic, does that mean the school's claim is invalid and it should stop doing whatever it is doing? Judging a program by what may be measured in its graduating students is useful but we must acknowledge that it is not the only way to judge the merits of a program.

Thus began our discussion of exit outcomes—learning goals. We wanted to be concise about what we expected of students. We wanted our students to have a clear idea of what they would need to do to graduate. And we wanted them to learn about it the day they walked into the school. We wanted to emphasize the notion of mastery, that students do not graduate merely by occupying a seat in class the minimum number of days and sliding by academically to accumulate credits. In every way possible we wanted to create a culture driven by the student's need to learn rather than the institution's need to look busy teaching.

In developing our learning goals, we also had an obligation to stick with the "New York State Goals for Students" as our guiding document. This document is a list of ten learning goals, developed by the New York State Board of Regents. It is intended as the guiding light for k-12 public education in New York State. Theoretically, all the state-developed curricula and commissioner's regulations flow from it and are developed in accordance with it. Therefore, early on in the design phase of the Lab School, we decided to adopt the list (we chose to not oppose it) as the guiding goal statement for the Lab School. The list would be a stabilizing force. It would be a stamp of officialdom we could point to when critics would accuse us of being a flaky alternative school.

Our learning goals discussion gradually worked its way through all of these issues, but it would have to be left to another session to generate a list that we could call our own. Meanwhile, we needed a math teacher. The kids were daily asking us, "Have you hired a math teacher yet?" And they were tiring of hearing our stock reply: "We're still working out the details." Two teachers were interested and ultimately one signed on—a first-rate teacher and great kid person who officially became the fourth member of our team in early March. Which was just in time for the potluck dinner.

We felt it would be beneficial to bring together all the Lab School families for an informal get-acquainted session. A potluck dinner in the school cafeteria seemed like a reasonable way to proceed. So we reserved the space, sent out invitations, bought some balloons, made a banner, and on a Tuesday night in March, conducted a festive gathering. A mixture of anxiety and eager anticipation was shared by all. We kept the formal portion of the program short with the teachers briefly introducing themselves and giving a short resumé; and other than that we just ate, mingled, and smiled a lot. We decided to not have a formal presentation of the curriculum, mainly because we didn't have one yet but also because we wanted this to be more of a community building event than an intellectual exercise.

Community. From the start, I envisioned the Lab School to be a community, and on many occasions in the design phase (and before) spoke of a sense of belonging that Lab School students—and teachers—might share. To skeptics, and to the skeptic's ear inside my own head, it sounded soft, even trivial. And when asked to explain what I meant by "community" and "a sense of belonging," I usually just made the idea murkier because I wasn't clear myself from an intellectual standpoint as to what it meant. I knew only that at certain points in my own life I had felt a part of a community and treasured those experiences, and I had observed at times groups of people who acted as a community. I knew viscerally what it meant but could not explain it.

Maybe it's like this: A community is a group of people who share a common purpose and who in working toward that purpose collaborate in meaningful ways. To be a community, people have to spend a lot of time together. They need to share more of themselves than merely the "business" side. They need to eat together, play together, laugh and cry together. They need to experience together a range of events and emotions. In so doing, a community is born.

What does it matter? Why is it important that a school be a community? Again, the answer does not have a hard edge, and to the skeptic it will sound soft and unpersuasive. Having lived with it now for a time and having witnessed its impact on students, the skeptic in me is indeed persuaded. It is important that a school be a community because when people feel a part of something they work harder and they care more. They want to do their best. It's that simple. One of the most common refrains of the embattled school teacher is that the kids just don't care and they just don't try. If a sense of community will eradicate those ills, then establishing it is worth a great deal of effort.

The Lab School has been criticized for diminishing "academic" class time in order to make room for the weekly "community meeting" (one period), weekly advisory group (one period), and weekly program (three periods). The critics are clearly penny wise and pound foolish. Though we lose academic class time, what we engender in motivation by building a community spirit more than compensates. I'd sooner teach a class three times a week to motivated students than five times a week to a group of kids who couldn't care less.

As winter turned to spring we were eager to meet with our students to be, and they with us. Any excuse would do. In April, we held an after-school meeting to discuss the selection of a theme for the coming year and to hear suggestions and concerns from the students as they faced their new program. I was struck with a realization impressed on me from two directions. The realization was that high school students need direction and structure. This should of course be assumed (and is) but its necessity was freshly affirmed. In developing our theme, we wanted to involve students so as to win their interest from the start (collaborating toward a common goal). We suggested that the purpose of the theme was to link the topics under study in the various courses. The theme would have to be broad enough to allow the inclusion of many diverse topics under its umbrella and rich enough to sustain (with interest) a year-long curriculum. It also had to be probing so as to encourage study in depth. Having explained all that, we led a brainstorming session with the kids. They had difficulty with the task. Together, they came up with a dozen or so possibilities such as "colors," "laugh," "differences." Mostly one-word, bullet-type headings. Too broad. They lacked the experience with curriculum development to really insightfully accomplish the task. They are students, after all. By definition, they lack experience. They need direction and structure. That is why there are teachers.

My realization came at me from a second direction. After the brainstorming session, we broke the students into smaller groups of about fifteen, and each teacher took a group to a classroom. There we sat the kids down and asked each to identify something they were looking forward to in the Lab School and something they feared or were anxious about. Each then shared their ideas with the group. Their comments about what they looked forward to were encouraging—a "sense of community," a "feeling of belonging" were frequently mentioned—but of more interest were their fears and anxieties. The clear, number-one fear was a lack of structure. They indicated that they needed in some ways to be guided, directed, not merely told what to do, but brought along gently. While many of our students to be had chosen the Lab School because in some way it represented freedom, freedom was also their greatest fear. Again, this should not be a startling insight to an educator, but to hear students explicitly address it affirmed its place as a guiding principle in our role as teachers.

Ultimately, the teachers chose the theme. We tried to draw on the conceptualizations of our students in the brainstorming session, but it was we who brought the theme to expression. After some discussion, cut short by a growing sense of urgency that it was May after all, and we needed to just start making some decisions (!), we settled on: "Diversity: weakness or strength?"

We each felt confident that the theme was applicable to our own discipline and, in particular, we liked the challenge that it put before the casual assertion that diversity is, of course, always a strength. What if it is not?

Our next opportunity to work directly with students was during a trip late in May to the Scarsdale Alternative School to observe a community meeting. Michele, Jane, and I were accompanied by four students picked in a lottery. Equipped with camcorder, bag lunches, and a box of Dunkin' Donuts for the ride, we made the three-hour trek south, the drive itself being a nice opportunity for students and teachers to share ideas. The community meeting we observed was an impassioned exchange over perspectives on drug and alcohol use. The crux of the discussion was whether school rules involving student enforcement of the district's drug and alcohol policy should extend off campus during weekends and evenings. Students were vigorously in favor of actively supporting the district's policy in school, indeed the A School had agreed to go beyond the policy by involving students in its enforcement, but the group's resolve broke apart once drug and alcohol use went off campus after school hours—some arguing for enforcement, others, against. The positions on this issue, while interesting, were not the most instructive aspect of our visit. Rather it was the nature of the discussion itself. This was not a classroom simulation of the democratic process. It was not a learning game or role play devised to teach students about critical thinking and decision making. This was the real thing. A real issue was being joined by real disputants who together had to come to terms with a real situation. While the A School teachers were frequent participants in the discussion, and while their comments to a large extent directed the course of the discussion, they were by no means the only people who spoke. Nor did students automatically agree with what the teachers had to say. On the trip home our students told us they were impressed that students ran the discussion and that everyone, including teachers had to raise their hands. Overall, we were all quite impressed by the community-meeting concept. That students and teachers should meet together each week to address and work toward the solution of vexing problems is a simple and potent opportunity to teach and to learn. What a shame that public education in America by and large overlooks it.

We returned home with our batteries charged, four very enthused students and some video footage to be edited for our upcoming evening session with Lab School parents and students.

By mid-May, we determined we had held off discussion of curriculum with parents about as long as we could. A kind of bargain had been struck after all. Fifty-four families (there were three late additions) had entrusted their children's education to us based on not much more than faith. We in return owed it to them to be open, honest, and informative. It was time for some information sharing.

The biggest news item was unfortunately not happy. Our math teacher was going to leave us even before we started. Her family had been unexpectedly presented with a once-in-a-lifetime opportunity to work and live abroad for two years. While she agonized over the decision for some time, she ultimately chose to go abroad since it clearly benefited her entire family. As soon as her decision was made, we got the word out to parents in a newsletter distributed in May. It was important that they hear it first from us. And it was also important to us that everyone know about it before the evening meeting. We did not want it to dominate the evening's deliberations.

At the meeting, we presented the newly adopted Lab School theme, and each of us gave an overview of the curriculum framework we were developing for our classes. Judy Wooster also presented her work with the college advisory group. She had recently received a number of replies to the latest mailing from the sixteen colleges and universities on our list. Their responses, which she shared with the audience, were positive and supportive. In general, the meeting, though much more businesslike than our last gathering (the potluck dinner), was upbeat. With one exception. In the course of the week, a number of students had made some comments about orchestra and choraliers (the school choral ensemble) taking place during second and fifth periods, respectively, next year. I hadn't paid heed to these comments because an agreement had been made that all the large music ensembles were to be scheduled third and fourth periods next year to meet the scheduling needs of Lab School students. Third and fourth periods were slotted for the visiting teacher classes. The day of the meeting, the issue came up with the principal who confirmed that, indeed, it looked like it was going to happen.

Having not yet had time to discuss the matter as a team nor having had an opportunity to discuss it at length with Dr. Hunter or the music department, I was not eager to bring it up at the meeting. But the rumor was out and a parent did indeed raise the issue, and we, falteringly said yes, it looked like it was true. Basically, we got cut off at the knees. In the days following, a scheduling compromise was reached whereby affected students would split their time between Lab School classes and music groups. Not an ideal arrangement.

With the curriculum meeting behind us, we began to look toward summer and the mountain of work that awaited us. It was all becoming real. Real kids, real parents, real issues, real deadlines. It was both terrifying and exhilarating.

Some reflections:

1. It is important to get away from your work. You will bring harm to yourself and everything you are working so hard to create if you do not occasionally get away from it all. Whatever opportunities to get away are afforded by your own particular circumstances, use them. We had a chance to head off to Key West while my parents took care of our girls. We could have quickly compiled a list of important things to do that week other than spending lots of money while getting no work done. But we went. Whether it's a hotel in Key West, a cabin in the mountains, or a motel with a pool across town, do it. Just do it.

2. Never ignore the concerns of colleagues; work through them as best you can, respecting that even if a concern seems silly to you, it is

clearly not silly to the person who raises it. Remember, not everyone shares your vision and goal. For them, the inconveniences and problems caused by what you are doing are not compensated for by the anticipation of that grand whatever-it-is. Indeed, to them, your "vision" may be seen as an individualistic, selfish ambition. Ignoring their concerns only proves them right. Grit your teeth and try to empathize. Your gestures toward fairness will generally be paid back in kind.

3. Address people, as well as issues. The Impact Committee certified the class-size issue as settled, but I feared that some colleagues were not "settled" about it. So I went to them and made sure. Matters are often worked out on paper without truly being worked out in peoples' hearts. Take the extra time to check in personally with individuals who seem least settled.

Political wisdom says to forget about the people who are most opposed and focus on the majority in the middle. Something in me has always made me focus on the extremists and, contrary to political wisdom, I think they should not be forgotten. Whatever it is that people generally oppose, they (the extremists) will be most able to articulate. If their reasons are legitimate, you had better attend to them. If their reasons are merely misperceptions or unfounded fears, inform them and reassure them.

4. Avoid trends and fads. Trends and fads are for people who don't think for themselves. Never allow yourself to be led by them. But don't ignore them. Look at them, identify the kernel of truth that usually lies at the heart of a fad, and if it is of value, make use of it. Identify also the layerings of stupidity that encase and obscure the truth. Leave all that aside.

5. Focus on results but beware of missing valuable experiences that don't always show up in results. Not everything that is valuable

can be measured. Measure what you can, discard what seems superfluous, but consider carefully the stuff that is neither: honesty, responsibility, character.

6. Communicate with your clientele. The best way to avoid ill feelings with clientele—both students and parents, but especially parents—is to build a foundation of good feelings through frequent communication. "Frequent" communication is relatively easy to achieve in public education, since the norm for communication is so very minimal. Indeed, anything that exceeds the usual quarterly report card and midperiod failing notice is an improvement that your parents will appreciate. In this phase of the Lab School's development, a couple one-page flyers and two meetings—the potluck supper and curriculum evening session—were our main means of communication. They helped to build a foundation of trust and respect without overburdening our emerging staff.

7. Build a community. This is a theme that I sound here and reprise in subsequent chapters. I cannot overemphasize its importance. Indeed, it is the essence of what a small school can do that makes it special. Our early meetings with parents and students established the relationship on which our community feeling would continue to grow. The trip to the Scarsdale Alternative School gave us a good sense of what we were striving for.

8. Students need guidance and structure. The word *instruction* implies the introduction of structure into the minds of one's students and is basic to education. The failure of some alternative school programs is, I suspect, due to the romantic and naive belief that young people are capable of establishing their own norms, goals, and procedures without adult guidance and without doing harm to themselves and others. I don't buy it. But neither do I accept the alternative extreme position that suggests educators ought to closely and rigidly

direct the students' learning without regard for the students' need to reason and explore on their own. As with so much else in life, moderation is key. Students need direction and prodding from adults and they need freedom to explore, make mistakes and perhaps draw some conclusions that, ultimately, might be at odds with the adults around them.

10. As much as possible, open your students to real experiences as opposed to simulations and games. I used to be a great believer in simulations and role plays as a sound learning device. I still think they have value; but why simulate and play roles when you can engage your students in the real thing? Lawrence Kohlberg found in some of his later work (based in part on studies of the Scarsdale Alternative School) that moral learning occurs much more effectively when people are faced with real issues and problems rather than hypothetical dilemmas. The simple commitment to student involvement in school governance opens a tremendous opportunity to engage in such *real* learning. And it should be an essential commitment of any school program.

The first indication that something was wrong came from Jean Franzcik,* our parent chaperone. She reported to us at breakfast that some kids might have been out of their cabins during the night. Within an hour the whole story was out, gathered from several sources, that while the teachers and chaperones for our beginning-of-the-year overnight conference slept, some (many? most?) of our students made merry in the night, ranging widely over the grounds of Camp Pinnacle, engaging no doubt in the full range of teenage after-dark-no-grownups-around sort of activities.

Camp Pinnacle is a church-affiliated family camp and conference center in the Helderberg Mountains west of Albany. When it is not hosting religious programs, it offers space to school groups. We had decided during the summer that an intensive retreat-like experience at the beginning of the school year might speed up the process of

---

* Parent and student names, throughout the text, have been changed.

community building and give us the chance to establish a different sort of school culture right from the start. We spent probably more time than we should have during our summer meetings fussing over the details of our two-day conference, but we wanted to get it right. It was crucial that this initial experience for our fragile, just-born program be positive.

Which is why we were rather upset when it came out that our new charges were engaging in a bit of deception during our trust-building adventure. Of course the thought crossed our minds, too, that when we got back to Delmar, the local grapevine would make our trip out to be some kind of drugfest free-for-all. When it was clear what had happened, Sue (our new math teacher), Jane, Michele, Jean, and I discussed options and agreed to confront the kids. So we postponed the morning's events (more trust-building exercises) and hauled all the kids together in our meeting room, where we confronted them. *We understand that not everybody honored the curfew last night.* Silence. *We are trying to establish trust here.* Silence. *We're working hard to create a different and exciting kind of program here. Are you just going to trample all our efforts?* Uncomfortable shifting. A hand goes up. *Yes, Erin.*

"I was out last night after the curfew and I'm sorry. I shouldn't have done it."

Silence. Another hand goes up. *Yes, Vicky.* "I was out last night, too. I'm sorry. I shouldn't have done it.

Two more hands go up. Another. Another. *Just how many of you were out prowling around last night?* Twenty hands go up.

"But Mr. Nehring"—this is Erin again, first to confess—"we really didn't do anything. We were just talking and getting to know each other."

Then Paul. "Yeah, like, we really didn't do anything. You know? I mean it was like a beautiful night and we just wanted to kind of like hang out." More comments to this effect. Then, just as the room was starting to loosen up, Jane cut in. "All innocent. Just talking. Going for a walk. Do . . . you . . . realize . . . Do you have any idea . . . the position you put us in as the adults responsible for your welfare while you are on this trip? What if, god forbid, something happened while you . . ." etcetera.

In the end, the kids owned up that it was not a cool thing to have done. We acknowledged that in the future we might involve them in the planning and making of rules—such as curfew. And, as a result, we all became somewhat closer. This unfortunate event, as it turned out, became a real positive. You cannot engineer a fall from grace and subsequent restoration. But sometimes it just happens. In our case it was a turning point. There was now a bond of respect between students and teachers. We respected them for confessing their error (with some assistance). They respected us for being concerned—even if the concern was partly for our own necks. It was a start. When we left for Camp Pinnacle Monday morning we were not yet a team. When we returned Tuesday, late in the afternoon, we were on the way to becoming a community.

The good thing about team building is that it can serve as sort of goodwill capital that you spend when times get tough. The first month of school saw two phases in our evolution as a school. In the first phase, the teachers became frustrated. In the second phase, the students became frustrated. We spent some of our capital.

We had decided during the summer that we needed to lay down a base of study skills and good work habits before getting into the academic routine. What we failed to appreciate was that unless our kids felt an urgent necessity for study skills and good work habits, all our preaching and teaching would fall on deaf ears. By and large, it did.

Michele, leading a workshop on time management: "I want you each now to take your personal calendar and draw lines across the week for each hour up through the weekend." Kids drew lines. It was not threatening yet. "Now, I would like you please to fill in what you plan to do during your after-school time between now and Friday and then fill in each of the hours for the weekend."

"What?!" exclaimed several students in unison. Murmuring from around the room.

"Do we have to like put in when we're going to the bathroom?" Scattered laughter.

"I have no idea what time I will eat breakfast on Saturday."

"I plan to fart at 3:15 Sunday afternoon." Riotous laughter. This was not working.

My own seminar on SQ3R (a technique for maximizing reading comprehension) met a similar fate.

"So you mean like we gotta do all this stuff, just to read some like ten-page homework assignment?"

I replied, "In the long run it will save you time—even if it takes more time up front—because you'll know the material well the first time you read it."

"Yeah, but like if I've got four homework assignments there's no way I'm gonna sit and do all this for each one. I can't. There's no time."

"That's where Ms. Atallah's time management workshop comes in." I chirped.

"Right."

Thus we workshopped and seminared the kids for three days. Not all were hostile and unreceptive. There was a substantial minority who took it as a kind of foreboding of the work load to come and paid attention. But the students who most needed it were going to have to learn the hard way.

Meanwhile, the faculty room was all curious about the Lab School. What the hell is going on up there in that classroom? Our opponents didn't ask. Our supporters, at lunch, haltingly, would say, "So . . . ?"

So we faced for the first time what to say in the faculty room about the Lab School. Our supporters were encouragingly interested, and we probably worried ourselves too much over what the skeptics would make of our comments. As it turned out, we didn't speak up a lot, partly out of timidness but mostly out of fatigue. By the time any of us staggered into the faculty room for lunch—assuming we were able to get away from our classrooms—we were so exhausted, it was just a lot easier to make small talk. We were finding early on that our full-time role as teacher was now augmented with a part-time role as politician—one we were unaccustomed to. There were to be some hard lessons in this realm over the coming years.

Our second full week of school brought the onset of real course work. Enough of this fluffy skills stuff! It was time to get down to academics! Oh that our students had been not only hearers of our workshops, but doers.

"This is just too much work, Mr. Nehring." This was Larissa during community meeting that week. "I mean I have never had this many assignments."

"Yeah, this is like very traditional. We thought Lab School was gonna be like innovative," said Tanya.

"You guys don't really expect us to do this, do you?" said Peter.

"We do."

And we did. First assignments came due. Some students turned them in. Many did not. Of those turned in, some were alright. Of those that were alright, only a few were really good. Our work was cut out for us. We started to lean on students in class. *Your work is not good. You're wasting your time. You're capable of much more. Push yourselves. Come on, you can do it.* The kids resisted, not with open opposition but by way of that time-honored kid approach—unruliness. They began to misbehave; showing up late to class, talking out of turn, not participating.

We held a team meeting. "What the hell," said Sue. "I mean what's the point of all this community meeting and advisory group and team-building stuff if the kids are just gonna give us the same crap as always."

"They're rebelling," said Michele. "Some of these kids joined Lab School because they thought it was going to be easy. Now they're finding out it's not easy, and they don't like that. So they do all this rebellious stuff."

"But that doesn't mean we condone it." said Jane incredulously.

"No, we don't condone it," Michele answered. "But it will pass. It's a phase. They're testing us."

The noncooperation continued. It went on outside of our classes, too, and the Lab School kids were beginning to get a reputation with the hall monitors. The visiting teachers, too, complained. The next week at community meeting I gave a this-behavior's-just-got-to-stop-damn-it lecture and the kids were momentarily stunned. Mr. Nehring, we didn't think you had it in you. Then something interesting happened.

Erin spoke. "You know, the teachers are right. I mean we can't expect that Lab school's just gonna be fun and games. It is school after all. And it *does* matter what people in the high school think about us." Some students rolled their eyes, but all were attentive.

"Erin's right." This was Jared. "I don't appreciate half the class screwing around while the other half is trying to pay attention. Some of us want to learn this stuff."

"You know it isn't as though the teachers are giving us little busy-work assignments either," said Paul. "I mean, you can tell they've really thought about their courses and are trying to like make them relevant."

The positive students were speaking up. And their comments had ten times the influence of the teachers'. The cut-ups looked shell shocked. They were being served notice by their peers. In the week that followed, however, classwide behavior did not noticeably improve. Cut-ups continued to cut up, only now under the disturbed countenances of their peers—who began to take recourse.

Student judicial council was a component of Lab School that we designed over the summer. In keeping with our mission statement, we sought to involve students in school governance matters. Rule making and rule enforcement were one area where clearly we could do that. I had attended a conference early in the summer at which I'd made the acquaintance of a principal in the Mid-west who ran a residential "governor's" school for gifted students. She told of an experiment conducted in one of their dormitories in which the usual long list of rules was discarded and replaced with a much shorter and more comprehensive list of just three rules: (1) take care of yourself; (2) take care of each other; (3) take care of this place. My principal friend reported that the short list worked. In the course of our summer Lab School teacher meetings we decided to try the same approach. Then, to enforce the rules we devised the Student Judicial Council. Whenever a member of the Lab School, student or teacher, felt a rule had been broken, he or she could refer the matter to the Student Judicial Council. The Council would be composed of a number of students who with one teacher would hear the case, determine by consensus whether a rule had been broken, and impose a penalty.

It didn't take very long for the first case to come to council. Jake Vanderheyden, a junior, had an explosive personality. He also did not have a good history as a student. While his new Lab School environment seemed to be making a positive impact on him, he frequently disrupted class. He also seemed to have a romantic interest in Erica Sanford, which came out mostly in the form of teasing and taunting. One day in class, the teasing and taunting finally got to Erica, who promptly told Jake to lay off. Jake exploded, cursing and gesturing wildly, all in the midst of an otherwise quiet, teacher-led class. Erica brought Jake to Judicial Council. To our great satisfaction, all present were respectful of the process. Erica stated her case. Jake waited patiently to offer his rebuttal. Council members asked questions to clarify, then Jake and Erica were escorted out of the room while the council deliberated.

Larissa spoke. "I think he's like guilty of breaking rule two, but like I don't see where he broke one or three."

"Well, Erica didn't say he broke one or three, just two. Right?" asked Jared. All nodded. There was a pause. Jared continued. "So, is there anyone here who thinks he isn't guilty?" Jared clearly relished the judicial aura of this proceeding. Another pause. The kids all looked at each other.

"Well, like, I mean . . ." this was Larissa again. "Guilty is such a strong word." Larissa always spoke as though she had marbles in her mouth, a kind of mild valley-girl affect. "You know this is not like some courtroom thing. We're just a bunch of kids."

I felt the urge to make some wise teacherly remark like, Yes, but isn't our system of justice based on a jury of your peers and isn't part of our mission as a public school to prepare you for adult responsibilities? And if you don't start doing it now in real, consequential situations, how can we expect you to do a good job as adults in situations where the stakes are much higher? But I thought better of it.

"Yes, but Larissa," said Paul, quiet until now. "The whole idea of

Student Judicial Council is for us, the kids, to decide. I mean, it's a test. Are we mature enough to make a hard decision. If we're not, then they'll just go back to writing us up and going to see the assistant principal and all that."

"Right," said Jared. "So, everybody, is Jake guilty of breaking rule number two?" All assented. "So then what do we do about it?"

"We do not give him detention. Detention is so totally bogus. I mean, the school comes up with such totally uncreative punishments. Punishments should be a learning opportunity."

The conversation continued in this vein. While I was philosophically in agreement, I feared this "learning opportunity" might be a little too attractive, that any deterrent value might be entirely absent. But I was pleasantly surprised. In the end, the penalty was for Jake to compose a list of ten nonhurtful ways to express anger, get the list approved by a teacher, type it up, and give one copy to each teacher to have available in their classrooms.

Jake and Erica were called back into the room, the decision and the penalty were explained, then each member of the council made a brief personal statement to Jake to the effect that the decision was difficult, and they hoped the penalty would be seen as a learning experience and not merely a punishment.

Jake took his lumps and eventually (a little late) produced his list. A quiet word seemed to go out among the kids that Student Judicial Council was to be respected. The kids were going to take it seriously. In some classes, the kids started to settle down. Whether it was Student Judicial Council or peer pressure or simple resignation to an unavoidable fate was unclear. But they settled down. And we were happy. Second language and math, however, were still facing a fair amount of noncooperation.

Michele's second-language/second-culture classes were organized to maximize student interaction with the second language. The classroom was organized into seven stations among which students would rotate, spending approximately fifteen minutes at each station. There was a satellite TV with Spanish and French broadcasting, a computer with interactive software in French or Spanish, a table with magazines and newspapers for reading, a table for writing exercises, a table for conversation, a center with audiotapes, and more. It was a very student-centered class. If the student took advantage of it, Michele's second-language/second-culture class provided a rich learning experience through which one became immersed in the host language and culture. If you chose to waste your time with idle chatter or fool around, the usual elements of a teacher-centered class that held misbehavior in check (silence, inactivity, the teacher's authoritarian presence) weren't there.

We discussed the situation in team meeting and Michele wondered aloud if the structure of the class was untenable for fifteen- and sixteen-year-old students. I maintained that really Michele's class was the kind of student-centered class we were all striving for. Indeed, if we decided to abandon the format and replace it with columns and rows we would be taking a giant step back. We agreed we wanted to teach students to be responsible for their education. We did not want coercion as our main instructional tool. Jane was uneasy. We all were, but Michele determined to stick with it. The old ways of teaching language did not work with students reluctant to learn anyway. At the least, this approach would do no worse. In fact, we were already doing better, since many of the students in Michele's classes wouldn't be taking a second language had they stayed with the traditional program. At least with us, they were getting some exposure.

Then there was math. In the original Lab School design, math was envisioned as a kind of a helper subject to science, providing the intellectual tools necessary to conduct science experiments and solve scientific problems. As such, math got fewer periods per week than any of the other subjects. The secondary place that math occupied in the Lab School design and the weekly schedule sent a strong and most unfortunate message to the students. And Sue bore the brunt of it. Additionally, the design team had been persuaded that heterogeneous grouping was to be generally preferred. Though this was nowhere stated in the design document, the design itself implied mixing all kids together. This seemed to be working in humanities class and in science, but in second language (Spanish and French together) and math, it did not seem to be working out. In each math class, Sue had students who had struggled in the most basic ninth-grade math course just prior to starting with her along with students coming out of the most advanced sophomore class offered in the high school. And there were twenty-seven students in the class. It is likely the very sequential nature of math learning that makes a heterogeneously grouped math class so challenging even when a science or humanities class tends to work, in some respects thrive, under the same circumstances. In math class one simply cannot move on to trigonometry without understanding algebra. On the other hand, one could do fairly well with a unit of study on the civil war without solid competence in the Age of Jackson. Likewise, an understanding of mitosis was not essential to understanding the Krebs cycle. The very technical and precise, almost manual nature of mathematics seems to lend itself to direct instruction more than other subjects. All of these factors compounded together made our math program difficult. Sue was awash in unruly students.

And there were other areas where solutions still eluded us: community meeting and group work. The purpose of the community meeting from an instructional standpoint is to teach students about democratic government by involving them in the governing process. At a practical level, the meeting serves as a regularly scheduled forum to which students and teachers may bring any school-related issue. My private fear during the summer was that no one would bring any issues to community meeting and we would all sit around and get fidgety. I like to have a contingency plan and with a student run community meeting there is no contingency. Either it works or it doesn't. As it turned out, I needn't have worried. There was plenty to talk about during the early weeks. We discussed Student Judicial Council, workload, homework policy, grading, Walkmans, drugs and alcohol use, relations with the high school, and more. What we had observed at Scarsdale was beginning to happen here. The students were beginning to take ownership of their education. They were being given power and they knew we were watching, waiting to see how they would use that power. I was not comfortable though with the structure of the community meeting—or lack thereof. While we were committed to the idea of a student-run meeting, we had no organized method of choosing a chairperson. And though we wanted everybody to feel free to bring the full range of issues to the community, we did not have a consistent procedure for establishing an agenda. Finally, there was no consistent follow-up. Issues were brought, discussed (sometimes heatedly), then dropped. In short, we needed more organization. We needed our own Robert's Rules. But we had to all feel the necessity of it first. That would come.

Group work. In the "real world," the world outside of school, people interact regularly in small groups, whether in the home or the workplace. In the workplace, especially, this is increasingly true. Groups can work well or poorly depending in large measure on the ability of group members to function as a cohesive unit. That takes practice and experience. Where better to gain the practice and experience than in school?

"Mr. Nehring, I really have to talk to you about something." This was Robin Delray. It was the end of the day, I had just dismissed my last class. We began to talk.

"It's not like I want to complain or anything, but like my group is just not working out. Erin and I do all the work and Phillip doesn't do a thing. He just sits there or fools around and the part we're supposed to do at home, he just doesn't do, and it's really unfair, and I know we're supposed to be learning how to work in groups and everything, but you know it just isn't fair that Erin and I do all the work and Phillip does nothing and we all get the same grade."

Robin was not the only student in my classes to complain. And in Michele's classes there were complaints about group work, too. This was a hard nut to crack. How would we create meaningful group work, that is a sort of project where the members truly had to rely on one another without including some measure of group accountability. While the grading system for many of our group assignments had an individual component and a group component, the bottom line was that a good student could suffer if her teammate failed to produce. And as much as we might insist that they needed to be assertive about getting all group members to pull together and how this is the way it is in the real world, it just was not entirely fair. We had to do something, but we were, as yet, unsure what that would be.

5

*Oct. 7, 1993*

*Dear Jon, Judy, and Les,*

*In anticipation of our getting together next Tuesday, I thought I'd pen a few preliminary thoughts. It's Thursday night, Laurie's offered to cover kids for the next half hour, so here we go . . .*

*Seen from shore, our little Lab School sloop is sailing briskly over the waves. The sails are trimmed, lines neatly coiled, and spray is flying across the deck as we make steady progress (blue skies, etc.). However, if you come aboard, and in particular, if you go below deck, you see the crew bailing madly while also stitching new sails, repairing splayed lines, patching leaks, charting the next leg of our course, watching the winds and weather, fixing the head, and hoping the swells don't get too ferocious as we head out into the open Atlantic with winter approaching.*

*We're holding our own, but we NEED some help.*

*First, we need some relief. Could you see your way clear to two days per quarter for each of us in the form of conference leave to regroup, plan for immediate events, and get our act together for next year when we will have seniors involved in all kinds of dazzling endeavors.*

*Second, the sound problem in 55-57 is debilitating. Michele and I both look forward to those occasional class periods when the other is not teaching on the other side of the wall. When we're both there we compete with each other until the noise is unbearable or our voices give out. Michele has laryngitis. We've got to do something. We've just got to. The kids are working on a solution as part of a project but it may be too little. Traveling is not the solution either. That will only create more stress as one of us races back and forth trying to beat the four-minute bell while keeping a cheerful demeanor for students. I would consider moving to another room if I had it all day.*

*Third, we need some administrative leave time built into our schedule next year to handle the INCREDIBLE amount of administrative work involved with keeping this program afloat. 0.4 FTE allocated not to one individual but to the teachers in general to be divided up in whatever way works best would be acceptable. We'd like to start talking about it as planning for next year is already upon us.*

*There's more but my half hour's up. We do look forward to seeing you on Tuesday, and I hope this letter doesn't scare you off! Overall, we're excited, upbeat, and doing well. We're just pretty stressed out.*

*Sincerely,*

*Jim*

By the fifth week of school we were all beginning to feel the stress. In addition to our Lab School classes we were each teaching two high school classes. For Michele and me this was manageable as we each had two sections of the one course. But for Jane and Sue it was intolerable. They each taught two different high school courses on top of their Lab School load. Some days, because of our rotating Lab School schedule, I would be with kids seven of eight periods during the day. If it was my turn to preside over Student Judicial Council my one free period, lunch, might get taken up, too. If there were after-school meetings—high school faculty meeting, Lab School team meeting, family conference—we could find ourselves burning straight from 7:30 in the morning when we opened our classrooms to 4:00 or 4:30, with no time to ourselves. On the light days, those days in the Lab School cycle that gave me a double period free, my time was fully absorbed by administrative activity. I confess to a naïveté about the administrative work load involved in a program like this. I had no idea how quickly and in what volume the administrative details pile up. I began dreading the trip to my mailbox, which regularly brought two to three crises per day. When was I expected to make all the phone calls, conduct all the meetings, and write all the memos just to keep the lines of communication open and this little program afloat? In hindsight, I feel sorry for my long-suffering teammates as some days I would arrive at team meeting utterly overwhelmed by everything that had to get done. I'd empty my pockets of phone messages, little folded notes to myself, urgent memos from guidance counselors wanting an immediate reply, having absolutely no idea where to begin. They were always most patient with me, considering that they had their own phone messages, folded notes, and urgent memos to deal with.

Why was there so much stress? It came from four sources really: (1) the fact that everything was new; (2) the fact that everyone was watching us; (3) anxiety originating with parents—just what had they gotten themselves into! (4) the complete absence of administrative leave time—we functioned in effect as a department without a supervisor or department head.

Everything was new: our grading system for example. High score was 6, low score 1. 4 meant proficiency and was equivalent to an 80 in the traditional grading system. In each course, the quarterly report card would show the handful of topics covered and the score earned for each. Furthermore, we said, a student had to score 4 or better in every topic in every course in order to graduate. What if a student scored a 3, how was it to be remediated? And what was to be our policy on late assignments? If we were truly dedicated to mastery, then it shouldn't matter if an assignment was late, as long as it was well done. But if we went that route, what would keep our students form procrastinating until it was too late to get the work done? We had to work out answers to all these questions.

Another example: double-period classes. Though we believed longer classes would benefit our students, it was an adjustment for them and for us. For the first few days, kids showed expressions of excruciating restraint as they marched back into the class they'd just left for part two. I found myself dazed and confused by the logistics of planning a double period, keeping the sequence of events straight in my head and consistent from section to section. And because there was so much to cover during that double period, there was an equivalent increase in the logistical questions from kids about when assignments were due and just what would be covered on the test and how long the essay was supposed to be and when the field trip money was due. It seemed that every time I paused to inhale, a student was either handing me some important piece of paper that had to go somewhere (immediately or be lost) or asking some question requiring a complicated answer.

And then there were the all-too-inadequate room dividers. Michele and I taught in a double sized classroom, often at the same time, each with a class of twenty-seven students. Between us stood five frail panels of fabric over rigid foam encased in a plastic and metal frame. Each stood seven feet high. The ceiling was ten feet and you could push the panels around, as they were freestanding. With three feet of open space between the ceiling and the tops of the dividers together with whatever vertical gaps occurred between the dividers, there was a great deal of sound leakage. Michele really did get laryngitis after the first month and we were driving each other nuts. Between my booming lectures and her satellite TV broadcasts (with fast-paced cartoon and game shows in the host language) it's a miracle our friendship survived. The kids, of course, were frustrated too. Noise from "the other side" was a constant distraction. We held a contest among our students for the best idea to solve the sound problem. Billy Alexander won and cleverly installed a high framework of PVC piping that effectively raised the height of each panel three feet to just below the ceiling. The idea was to then drape blankets over the framework for sound insulation. Unfortunately, it proved ineffective, partly because the blankets didn't muffle well enough and partly because we didn't have enough blankets to span the full forty feet of panels. In total frustration, Michele made arrangements with a sympathetic teacher across the hall whose room was free during the right periods to move her high school classes. That solved the problem for our high school classes (which was good as they had recently taken to throwing stuff—pencils, paper wads, feminine products—over the dividers), and for our Lab School classes we decided that since the schedule rotation had us teaching back to back only some of the time, we could endure.

In addition to everything being new, everybody was watching: teachers students, administrators, board members, the town. We were a fishbowl—an opaque fishbowl, which meant that since people couldn't see clearly everything that went on, they imagined what they could not see. What they imagined was the source of much gossip.

One evening I was approached at the town library by a woman who began by saying how exciting she thought the Lab School was and how difficult it must be for me to live in the shadow of such famous parents. What? Well, I mean to have a father who's a famous author and all. What are you talking about, ma'am? Well, I understand you're the son of Scott and Helen Nearing? No. Well, that's certainly the rumor going around town. It being the library, I looked up Scott and Helen Nearing and found out they were back-to-the-land anarchists from the 1930s who wrote books and ran a farm in Vermont. Great. This is what was going around town. The rumors about Camp Pinnacle, too, proved to be what we had feared. So, we were getting labeled as a pot smoking, anarchist, hippie alternative school. High school students, too, passed around the same rumor. When we asked our own students what they thought about the drug rumors, they confirmed that drugs were widely available in the Lab School—just as they were in the high school. Indeed, within the first several weeks of school we made several referrals of suspected drug use to the school counseling program. Which was ironic. We were being aggressive about a problem, refusing to sweep it under the carpet and our reward was to become grist for the local gossip mill. The lesson to be learned of course would be that if you pretend successfully that you have no problems, your school gets a great reputation as a wonderful "drug-free environment." It is a lesson we adamantly refused to learn. Near the main entrance to the high school stands a sign reading "Drug-Free Zone." Some clever disrespecter of signs has altered it to read, "Drugs for Free Zone."

I sometimes felt uncomfortable strolling into the faculty room. While most of our colleagues either quietly supported our work, or told us their concerns, or kept their opinions to themselves, there was a vocal minority who had concerns but did not bring them to us.

The greatest source of frustration, as a fishbowl school, were the mistruths that occasionally circulated: one, that Lab School was an unstructured free-for-all, and, two, that the teachers had it easy. To the first, let us understand something about structure. If by structure, one means coercive force applied at every moment for tasks that are excruciatingly detailed and monitored by the minute, then, yes, Lab School is not structured. If, however, by structure one means meaningful direction to students engaged in meaningful tasks with the goal of maximizing learning, then there is structure indeed. It is not the kind of structure one is accustomed to seeing in a traditional school. As to the second charge that Lab School teachers had it easy, this was so totally outrageous that whenever I heard it, always second hand, my blood would boil. And I would have to really work hard to keep from thinking uncharitable thoughts toward a few of my colleagues who had the uncanny ability to get their work done so speedily that they could reliably be seen drinking coffee in the faculty room, discoursing on the Lab School and how easy we had it.

Another source of stress was the understandable anxiety that exuded almost visibly from our parents. Sometimes we could answer their questions: Will we get report cards? Will there be grades? Do you give homework assignments? Other questions were more difficult: What does X college think about the Lab School? I tried always to be patient with unnerved parents. These were, after all, courageous people, entrusting their kids to a bunch of renegade teachers with stars in their eyes. They were showing tremendous faith in us and we, in reciprocity, owed them much. I think they understood that we didn't have all the answers but accepted it because we had shown them already that when the time came we would figure out—together—whatever needed figuring out.

The final source of stress was the fact that we were running this program as full-time teachers. We had no administrative leave time, as any other department would, and we had at least the same amount of administrative work to be done. Granted, we were not responsible for teacher evaluation, but in place of that were all the time-consuming tasks associated with a new program.

These complaints are important to chronicle but they can become self-indulgent. After all, I had worked hard to get myself into the stressful and rewarding position I now faced. As a teacher friend who had observed the development of the Lab School sometimes reminded me: "Be careful what you wish for because you may get it."

Student evaluation is an area where we wanted to tear down the traditional methods and get creative. During the previous summer I had attended a conference sponsored by RJR Nabisco for education entrepreneurs—people from all over who were striking out in new directions in public education. There I met Dennis Littky, principal of Thayer High School in Winchester, New Hampshire. We were talking at dinner about standards and how to sell the graduates of high school programs that didn't employ the usual standardized tests to colleges that necessarily had to compare one program with another. Dennis talked about one promising senior at his school who wanted to attend M.I.T. What would M.I.T. know about a little rural public school in New Hampshire? Not much. So, Thayer High School invited an admissions representative from M.I.T. to observe the student's senior presentation. If he was impressed, it would no doubt bode well for the student's admission.

This conversation percolated in the back of my mind during the weeks that followed. It intersected at some point with another thought. It seemed that whenever we talked up the Lab School at outside functions, community members would frequently offer in a vague sort of way to "help out" if we ever needed them. The offers were sincere, well intending, but not of much use.

An idea emerged. What if we called in all those offers by asking members of the community to observe and help evaluate, on a regular basis, our student presentations. We could create a kind of Board of Examiners. Accomplished professionals and prominent citizens from around the community who would come to the Lab School for a half day to evaluate our students' midyear and end-of the-year oral presentations. We developed the idea during our summer curriculum meeting, and before school began in September we had mailed out nineteen invitations to prominent local figures with whom we had some connection: our state assemblyman, a General Electric scientist who had worked with the Lab School design team, all of the members of our Board of Education (accomplished professionals in their own right), several admissions officers at local colleges (Skidmore, Union, RPI, Hudson Valley Community College), a writer for the Albany newspaper, and others. Within several weeks of the opening of school we heard replies from all, almost without exception in the affirmative. We had tapped into a latent resource.

Having succeeded in assembling an impressive board, we felt now under considerable pressure to ensure that our students performed suitably. Such pressure is a good thing. We had a personal stake in preparing our students for their exams. We didn't want to embarrass ourselves. Also, with outside "neutral" parties serving in the examination process, our students were thus advised that they could not rely on any preexisting relationship with their teacher to help pull them through a weak performance. They would be examined by people they had never met. The incentives were right.

Once we had passed through the initial several weeks of stabilizing and acclimatizing, our attention turned to the exams, the first round of which would occur at week twenty. There was much to be done. Actually, to say our attention turned to it is not wholly accurate. I sometimes liken our operational mode in Lab School to a crisis team called on to respond to many crises at once. Every time a crisis arises a red light flashes on some control panel in front of us. While we have the ability to address maybe three or four crises at a time, there are usually a dozen red lights flashing. At about four weeks the Board of Examiners red light began silently to flash, joining an already brightly lit board. When we noticed it at week five, we scrambled desperately to do all we could, amid all the other crises, to get the exam process together.

At the end of September, we announced to our assembled students that we would conduct trial exams during week seven, and that to prepare they would each write a short (for them long) 750-word research paper to be submitted in advance, then orally presented and defended in a live forum. At that our students' backs straightened. There was more, we said. In addition to being knowledgeable about their own work, we explained that they must also read and understand well the work of their group members—we had assigned them to groups of three—as the examiners could ask them questions based on their teammates' papers. More back straightening. We were doing this, we said, because we wanted them do a good job for the examiners, during the "real thing." This last statement produced an especially satisfying result because it presented us (teachers) as not the bad guy for imposing all this work, but the kind and concerned helper, the coach, for wanting to get the team in shape for the big tournament.

The trial exams turned out to be a useful experience, if rather chilling. The kids went to work writing their reports—without enough guidance from us—then submitted multiple copies for their teammates and one teacher. We had decreed that each group of three must produce one humanities paper, one second-language paper, and one math/science paper. Thus each student would be responsible for knowledge in all three core disciplines. The orals were held during a weekly program that extended to a second day. For the most part, students were very nervous, read almost entirely from their written report for the oral presentation, and were almost wholly ignorant of each other's papers. We explained with patient insistence that this simply would not do. The written reports were no better, being merely descriptive with virtually no interpretation, analysis, opinion making, or personal reflection. We consoled ourselves as teachers with the rationalization that the dearth of cultivated intelligence present in the trial exams was a reflection of ten years of questionable effort on the part of our students and not the result of seven weeks of impoverished education on the part of the Lab School teachers. Give us three years with these kids and we'll turn them all into marines!

We pressed on, determining to do another round of trial exams at fourteen weeks. One of the great joys of the Lab School, which we discovered and began to fully exploit early on, was the flexibility of our schedule. For three-fourths of the school day, we were completely autonomous. That is, with the exception of periods three and four when our students attended phys. ed. and their visiting teacher classes, it was strictly the four permanent Lab School teachers interacting with fifty-four students. If we chose to suspend afternoon classes, it was purely our decision. If one of our two sections got ahead of the other due to a holiday or a reordering of periods the previous day to accommodate a special program, we could easily adjust by flipping sections around or shortening classes from double periods to single periods. We did this easily, almost recklessly, in the early weeks, drunk with our new freedom. And we paid for it. Kids were starting to get confused about the schedule. They'd show up in one classroom, any classroom, for first period and ask plaintively, hollow-eyed, Where am I supposed to be? Then there would be a wave of group migration as kids fled toward the right rooms. They also learned to use all this rescheduling to their advantage: *I didn't read the short story because when you assigned it on Monday we weren't going to have you until Thursday and now its only Wednesday and all of a sudden here we are. So, like, I didn't do it.*

We learned after the first couple of months to announce schedule changes in advance, to post the changes, to ask in advance whether anyone had questions, and then to not take any excuses about homework not being done. Once we had the game mastered and managed to be less slaphappy about rescheduling, our flexibility became an asset. If an important weekly program ran overtime on Wednesday afternoon, we continued Thursday morning and condensed our Thursday classes to one period. This is truly one of the great virtues of small size: that we can reconfigure our learning activities to meet the always evolving and sometimes unpredictable needs of our students. Whatever we lose by scaling down, we more than make up for with this asset alone.

One such unpredictable learning need came to pass about a month into the school year, and it arrived in the form of a letter from Camp Pinnacle where we had conducted our beginning-of-the-year conference. The letter stated that the Lab School was being levied thirty dollars to cover the cost of a broken lamp, torn sofa, and two chairs left out in the rain. Furthermore, the letter chastised the Lab School in general for being poor stewards of Camp Pinnacle facilities. We were not amused, and without a great deal of prior reflection on our part (the teachers), we presented the letter to our students at community meeting the day it arrived, which happened to be a Wednesday. After reading the letter, we opened the floor for discussion. The first comment came from Phillip Sisco: "Well, I don't see as we need to get all upset about it or nothin'. I mean these things happen. You take fifty people anywhere and there's bound to be some stuff that gets broken. I mean, it happens. So we'll send 'em thirty bucks and say thank you for bringing it to our attention. You know, I mean I don't think we need to get upset about it." Phillip was looking for nods of agreement from around the room and wasn't finding many. Other students spoke up saying what a shame it was that they had to send a letter like that and how we ought to write an apology.

I spoke. "I agree that its really unfortunate that Camp Pinnacle had to deal with this problem, especially after they were very hospitable to us and gave us such a good rate. And, Phillip, I sure hope that every time we take you guys on a field trip we don't have to expect that you'll all leave a wake of destruction in your path. If we do, then I won't support field trips." Pause. "I think what we need to do is to pay the thirty dollars, write the letter of apology and something else . . . I think we need to show that we're embarrassed about this and we need to do something to make it right. I mean, what if we all went up there some Wednesday afternoon and volunteered to do some work, maybe clearing trails or raking leaves, something like that." With this idea on the table, some fairly responsible students picked it up and talked favorably about it. We continued our discussion for the remainder of community meeting and by the end had agreed by consensus that we would make a return trip to do work and that we would do this not as a way of punishing everybody for the misdeeds of a few but as a statement that we as a school cared about our reputation. Camp Pinnacle was very receptive when I called later that afternoon to the idea of our returning to do work. I was put in touch with Emilio who said he could put together six or seven projects if we could divide our kids into work details of seven or eight persons. We ordered up some buses, sent home permission slips, and the following Wednesday made the half-hour trip up the mountain. I feared that given the mere two hours of real work time that we had, we'd do no more than make a mess of whatever projects we began. But the kids surprised me. Emilio was ready for us and when we sent the students off in their work details, they got right down to business. In two hours they raked a large yard and loaded a dump truck full of leaves, painted two bathroom floors, cleaned the kitchen, organized some office materials, moved two truckloads of split logs and cleared a trail. The staff was ecstatic, and we left in high spirits.

One important element in the success of our return trip to Camp Pinnacle was that we had agreed to it by consensus. We found, in the course of these early months that decisions made by consensus served us all well. We benefited greatly by the presence of a consensus expert in our midst. Jane, in addition to being an outstanding teacher, was also trained in consensus-based decision making and had experience teaching consensus skills to groups. At our initial Camp Pinnacle conference she led the students through several hours of training. The kids liked the fact that everyone's opinion counted and we liked that no one could hide. Everybody had to make their views known and be prepared to defend them. The necessity of negotiation and compromise, as well as the verbal and thinking skills associated with the process, provided in itself excellent training.

Our consensus orientation highlighted for us a dilemma, though. We wanted, on the one hand, to promote democratic governance in our school as much as possible. Consensus honored that commitment. On the other hand, there were occasions when we as teachers wanted to reserve our right to make decisions without student veto power. As consensus highlighted this dilemma, it also provided a solution. As issues came before the community meeting it gradually became clear that they tended to fall into two categories: school environment decisions and curricular decisions. The decision to return to Camp Pinnacle was of the former category and we felt comfortable leaving it to consensus. A matter such as homework (i.e., how much) was of the latter category, and we did not want students dictating to us that we could or could not give homework. As the weeks passed and more such distinctions were made and as we discussed with our students the nature of the difference, we began to feel comfortable identifying issues as one category or another, and said so at the beginning of a discussion so that our students would know at the outset whether they would be actually making the decision or only providing input and influence on what would ultimately be a teacher decision.

Thus the early weeks tumbled by, our relationship with the students grew and deepened as we faced so many issues together for the first time. We were indeed beginning to come together as a community. As our relationship with our students grew, we felt it crucial to establish a strong relationship with parents.

In most conventional high schools parent-teacher relationships are mostly nonexistent. The high school PTA in most schools is peopled by a handful of committed stalwarts who, try as they may, generally exercise little influence in school matters. At the classroom level, a student's daily experience is diffused among so many different teachers that there is no single one to whom a parent may turn for any real overview of their child's progress. The guidance counselor, responsible for maybe 250 students cannot, try as she may, provide the kind of authoritative, personal, in-depth knowledge of a student's situation that a parent desires. Communication between home and school is indeed thin, consisting of a quarterly report card showing a number grade, possibly some computer-generated comments and optionally a midquarter progress report four times a year with a short explanation as to why a student is failing. Teachers, overwhelmed by mountains of paperwork will tend to use the midquarter progress report forms to indicate impending failure as a preemptive measure against a parent who might later charge that he or she "did not know."

Face-to-face meetings between teacher and parent are indeed rare. Back-to-school night, the only regularly scheduled parent-teacher meeting, brings parent and teacher together for all of about ten minutes. Those ten minutes allow the teacher just enough time to provide an overview of their course. The parent is granted a brief opportunity, as one senior colleague used to say, "to see the body" (referring to the teacher). Given the ultra-stiff nature of back-to-school night, a cadaverous analogy is apt.

The only other face-to-face meeting occurs as a case conference in which all teachers assemble to meet with parent(s). The guidance counselor serves as host and M.C. This is usually an ultra-ultra-stiff affair as the usually negative events that have prompted the meeting have by this stage created a dire situation. Thus the first real sit-down discussion occurs in a climate of crisis. There is usually no prior relationship among the parties that would establish a foundation of trust. All around there is apprehension and often some level of distrust. You didn't keep us informed. Your child is out of control. Your teaching methods are bad. You just need to exercise more discipline at home. Thus what should be an alliance in the interest of the child can become target practice with blame for bullets.

We were determined to eradicate this pathology as part of the Lab School's mission. At the same time, we were committed to doing so without greatly expanding the work obligations of our teachers. In the end, we would find that "greatly" is a crucial modifier. Indeed, reflecting on our experience it is impossible to envision a program such as ours with teachers who would put in the contracted thirty-seven and one-half hours. Utterly impossible. I would judge that with the program fully operational, teachers would have to plan on at least a fifty-hour week.

Is this fair? Is it realistic? Fairness, the issue often raised by skeptics, is not the central one (though it is not entirely peripheral) for those of us most closely involved. For us, excellence has been the key issue. And excellence simply cannot be achieved through ordinary effort, whether the setting be public school, for-profit corporation, government agency, or small business. There is always struggle, risk, sacrifice, and the attendant anxiety in the pursuit of excellence. But as long as there is also reward—personal satisfaction, recognition, respect, appreciation, freedom, and a reasonable salary, it is worth it. The Lab School requires unusual effort and commitment by its teachers to remain what it has become, but in any institution striving for excellence, the employees will display and will be expected to display those same qualities. In my own school district, those programs, courses, and teachers, with excellent reputations have labored and continue to toil to maintain their reputations. Institutions are never excellent; people are. Institutions may create the conditions that promote excellence, but people must always toil and sacrifice to achieve it. The equation is nothing new.

Establishing parent-teacher relationships began even before our students signed up. The promotional material and evening informational sessions were all exercises in trust building. Our clients needed to trust us before they would commit their children to our care. That, in itself, gave us a jump start, and that is also a good argument in favor of giving parents the opportunity to choose from among more than just one school program. When the family chooses the program, the relationship begins with confidence.

Our efforts to build the relationship continued through the spring months after course sign up with the potluck dinner in March and evening curriculum session in May. During the summer months as we developed the program further, we tossed around the idea of a newsletter, something that could be sent out on a more or less regular basis whenever there was a mailing home. I had just purchased a laptop computer and the software included a simple desktop publishing program. It seemed like a manageable possibility—if the newsletter could be kept short, say front and back sides of a single sheet with double columns, produced entirely on the laptop, printed on our in-house printer, and duplicated on our in-house copier. We spent more than a reasonable amount of time coming up with a name. We made a great list and, as these things go, got a little punch drunk ("Fungus among-us") as the list grew without a name that hit us all right between the eyes. Ultimately, I began producing the first issue before we had a name and at a moment when I was not thinking about it, one suggested itself: FUTURES. And thus it has been since our first issue, dated August 1993. This is what appeared in that first issue by way of explaining the name.

> *"FUTURES" implies several ideas. First is the future orientation of the Lab School, which seeks to prepare students for life in the next century (now looming imminently). Second is the anticipation that new ways of teaching students well, pioneered here in the Lab School, will catch on and spread. Finally, and most importantly, are the futures of our students, your children, who have been entrusted to our care.*

As an afterthought on production, a great time-saver has been the practice of conceiving and composing the articles and text right in the columns of the newsletter format so that writing and production are collapsed into one unified and timesaving step.

The newsletter has served us well. We have attempted to keep it newsy and upbeat as well as an open conduit for some of the less pleasant but important information and commentary.

One of the early occasions for the publication of FUTURES was the end of the first marking period—a landmark event for our new program. What is most memorable about that period is the enormous amount of time that was required to fill out and mail our fifty-four first-quarter report cards. The report card design that evolved over several years from our early experiences takes only a little more time than a traditional report card to complete, but our first attempt was simply unmanageable. It was the first time through, and our critics delighted in pointing it out as yet a further example of the unmanageability of our program within the normal bounds of accepted workload.

The production of our first report card involved approximately forty-eight person hours—weighting assignments, determining averages, conferencing over interdisciplinary grades— plus seventy-five hours of clerical time, forty hours of which was conducted by a clerk typist hired (after much pleading to the district) to help us out, and thirty-five hours by Michele who would have worked around the clock if not for the sensible intervention of her dear husband George!

The Lab School report card was, at that time, in a two-page format listing the five Lab School goals and under each a handful of subgoals. The five graduation goals are for the student to demonstrate proficiency as: (1) an adept thinker and problem solver; (2) an able communicator; (3) a capable and committed citizen; (4) a confident and mature individual; and (5) a capable scholar in a range of academic disciplines. Before describing the report card, a detour into the origin of the five goals. From our earliest discussions, central to the Lab School design was the concept that goals would be clearly defined and that mastery of them would be truly the driving force behind all student and teacher efforts. Rather than base our graduation criteria on a system of credits earned, accruing as a kind of proxy toward graduation, we sought to hold our students accountable directly to our graduation goals. Our five goals were derived from the New York State Learning Goals for students in kindergarten through twelfth grade. One might ask why we didn't just use the goals verbatim: too unwieldy. The New York State goals, like so much developed by the State Education Department, are as much an effort to please multitudinous constituencies as they are an effort to produce educationally sound material. As a consequence of the former, the document's clarity is seriously compromised. We did not want to adopt the same gobbledygook sort of language, so we began with the New York State goals and trimmed away the excess verbiage.

On page one, we listed goals one through four with a separate line for each subgoal. This is where we encountered our first difficulty. We had been teaching our classes in some respects like traditional courses with course objectives, and so forth, but we had not explicitly tied our course objectives to our graduation goals. A serious mistake. So when we turned to evaluating our students on their progress toward the various subgoals, we found ourselves reaching to connect a subgoal with some class activity or other school event in an after-the-fact sort of a way. Eventually, we were able to do it and we could justify every score we gave should a student or parent question us. But it took an enormous amount of time and just didn't feel right to be sorting this all out after the fact.

Page two of the report card displayed scores for goal number five ("competent scholar in a range of academic disciplines"). This part of the report card was more traditional, showing scores for each subject area. The only difference was that each subject area instead of showing just one score for the marking period showed anywhere from three to six or seven based on the topics covered. Here scores were easier to determine and easier to justify as they were directly tied to classroom activities and assignments.

Thus exhausted by our report card ordeal and with all report cards deposited in the mail box, we left school on Friday afternoon, the last day of the first quarter, and repaired to Michele's house with our dear, long suffering spouses and companions, where we uncorked a bottle of Riems champagne. We then retreated to a restaurant and dance club far from Albany, so as to ensure complete anonymity and made merry eating, drinking, and dancing until 3 A.M. We had survived the first ten weeks!

The report cards must have hit home between Saturday and Monday because the phone messages appeared in our mailboxes beginning Tuesday, together with the concerned and upset looks from our students. We had been frank in our appraisals, particularly in the first four goal areas. The problem was that students were unaccustomed to being told in a formal, written report that they were something less than "a confident and mature individual" or "adept thinker and problem solver" or "capable and committed citizen." They were accustomed to being told they passed or failed a particular subject. This was a shock and the charges of "unfair" and "how do you know" and "how can anyone judge another person in these areas" began to mount. To the general feeling of shock we responded that Lab School is different and if Lab School truly values the items we list as our goals, then they are what we must rate our students on. To the more substantial question of what our ratings were based on (how does one judge confidence and maturity?), we pulled out our notes on each student. We took pains to explain—in class, in community meeting, on the phone—that our judgments were based on what the student had demonstrated, or failed to demonstrate in our presence or in Lab School work, with respect to each goal, that is, if we judged a student as lacking in confidence and maturity it was a statement that he or she hadn't shown it to *us*. This helped not only in salving wounds to the ego, but also unintentionally in suggesting a revision to the report card. Told that she hadn't demonstrated maturity to us, the student tended reasonably to query, How then may I show it to you? It was a perfect opening to craft some kind of project or learning activity. The students were asking for it. The full meaning of both the report card format's impracticality and the opportunity to revise it, however, did not hit us until after the second quarter. More will be said about that later.

As we hit bumps in the road such as the mild rancor over the report card, the potential for strain between parent and teacher and student and teacher was held in check by the foundation of trust that had been established. If some parents began to seriously question their involvement with this new program, their misgivings were counterbalanced by the thought that *these are good, caring teachers. I've met them. I know them. I trust them to work this out.* There was shared history, an established relationship.

There was going to be a delicate balance to our relationship with parents, as we were beginning to discover. On the one hand, we wanted and needed their support—mainly for the academic success of their child but also for the sake of the program. On the other hand, we needed to insist on quality academic standards, which insistence could make parent-teacher relationships at times quite bumpy. The team had numerous intense conversations on just this point around the time our ten-week report cards went out and we all agreed that we would insist on our standards even if it meant the death of the program. If we were going to succeed, our success would be meaningful, not hollow. This shared sentiment pumped us up with courage and gave us sufficient moralistic bravado to face the challenges that lay ahead. To wit, we feared some kids might bail out and that if a few bailed out, more might follow and that we would shortly find ourselves hemorrhaging students. We did not want this to happen, so we needed to ask ourselves whether our determination to keep a student from leaving would be driven by our fear of losing the program (the wrong reason) or by our desire for what was truly best for the student.

Our first opportunity to face all these abstractions in the flesh came with Robert Bojet. Robert was accustomed to just getting by in school. He had achieved passing grades over the years without great effort and was content with that level of achievement. We were not. We wanted more of Robert. He was, in our estimation, bright and capable of far more than he allowed himself. The academic results of his first quarter's work were mixed. He had done well enough with some work proving that, indeed, he was capable. But in other areas there were great holes, suggesting he had more or less chosen to not make the effort there. His work overall would have earned him minimally passing grades in the regular program but the Lab School insisted on mastery. Our first parent conference was held in November shortly after report cards went out. Robert's father suggested we were asking too much, that all this work and all these demands were demoralizing to a lad of sixteen. He came very close to saying that just getting by ought to be good enough. We urged, in positive, encouraging tones, that Robert was indeed capable, that he had demonstrated he was capable—just look at his work (we brought samples)—and he, you, Robert just needed to believe in yourself and your ability to excel. Could Robert transfer out of the program came the inevitable question. That really was not a very attractive option we suggested, pointing out that (a) academically Lab School was an appropriate setting for Robert—he had demonstrated he could do the work—and (b) because the Lab School curriculum was so different, transferring back to the high school might mean losing a semester or a year; and that (c) Robert could make it in Lab School, he just needed to put forth the effort and give it some time. Both father and son had come into the meeting entertaining the inclination that when it was over, Robert would be out of Lab School. We were pleased they left otherwise, but wondered if Robert's new resolve would last.

As the parent calls and student discussions multiplied in the week or two after report cards went out, we determined that we ought to do something on a schoolwide basis to address parent and student concerns together. A friend who works in politics once cited to me a formula that for every piece of constituent mail received, one may calculate, there are two hundred other constituents, like-minded, who did not bother to write. Enlightened with this thought we decided our notion of a schoolwide something or other might just be a good idea.

Here we face a conundrum. Excellence takes dedication and time commitment. Some of our more ardent union colleagues had warned against setting precedents—for a lengthened workday or other new job responsibilities—that might be called to the attention of the union negotiator at contract-bargaining time. At the same time, there were many teachers not at all associated with Lab School who put in enormous amounts of time setting up science labs in the late afternoon, coming in Saturdays and Sundays to evaluate student art projects, giving up school vacations to work with students on extracurricular projects like the student newspaper or literary magazine, making phone calls to parents in the evenings, the list goes on. Rarely did these activities become the focus of intense union discussion as our nascent efforts were rapidly becoming.

We needed clearly to extricate ourselves from all this distress. So it came to us one bright morning ( I think it was Jane's idea): Why not hold a Lab School breakfast? We could hold it on a Thursday morning during periods one and two in place of our usual advisory group session. Parents, students, and teachers would all meet together for coffee and donuts and an open forum for discussion of whatever was on people's minds. As we thought about it, it dawned on us that such a breakfast might help loosen the conundrous knot of circumstances we currently faced. Holding it during school would strike any charge that we were lengthening the work day. Also, periods one and two, approximately 8:00 to 9:30, were timed well for working parents who could go conveniently from home to Lab School breakfast to work, arriving only slightly late to work. Additionally, early morning would catch everyone fresh as opposed to the usual evening slot reserved for school meetings when folks are generally tired and easily liable to become ornery. As well, holding the breakfast during advisory block assured us of full attendance by our students while avoiding any disruption of our academic schedule.

Thus rejoicing in our clever solution, we went ahead. Of our fifty-four students, some thirty-four were represented by one or two parents. The agenda was open. Teachers sat down front, parents and students in the ascending lecture hall rows of desks. The layout was actually a tactical error, as it suggested a division—teachers against parents and students—but the meeting went well nonetheless. We were pleasantly surprised that despite all the concern about grades, not one parent implied that we should back off our standards. We kept up a steady stream of you-can-do-it and just-make-a-consistent-effort, all of which seemed to resonate well with our parents because it is what they already believed about their children. I shared at the breakfast an observation I had made during the first marking period, an observation based on my dealings with the very diverse student body of the Lab School and the entirely heterogeneous (read random) assignment of those students to my humanities class. The observation: variation in achievement from student to student appears to have little to do with innate intelligence (whatever that is) and more to do with confidence and work ethic. I'd observed students who in my casual judgment were not the brightest or swiftest in the verbal realm but believed in their efforts and worked hard and achieved well. At the same time, I'd observed students who had tremendous verbal ability and for whatever reason seemed to have little faith in themselves, made little effort, and fell on their faces academically. Confidence and work ethic are two areas that students under the direction of a competent teacher and a caring parent can improve upon. Thus, I wished to emphasize to all assembled, academic success is up to us, it is within our power and not merely the determination of a genetic toss of the dice. I believe this is true for nearly all students that find their way into public high school. This is, as I said, what parents already believe and what they want to hear. Statements to the contrary tend to arise when there is a need to go on the defensive, lay blame, make excuses for a lack of success.

Not until teaching in the Lab School did I come to this opinion with such certitude. Working with students who exhibited such diversity of ability, achievement, and maturity, it all became quite clear. I doubt I shall ever be persuaded otherwise.

We took good notes at our first breakfast and indicated that we would take all comments and suggestions to heart—which behooved us to make at least some changes or a public explanation of why there would be no change if we wished to maintain the credibility that we were beginning to enjoy.

The level of anxiety I had imagined present among parents did not seem to materialize at the meeting. It wasn't clear whether it was faith on their part that we would work things out, fear of speaking up in a large group, or simply no real anxiety to begin with. Perhaps the truth lay somewhere between. There was concern among some parents that the Lab School was earning a reputation as a program for kids who couldn't fit in elsewhere, who couldn't function in the regular program. We responded that each of us is our own best ambassador and it is up to us to set the record straight. The parents were, apparently, feeling the weight of the old "alternative school" reputation that was so hard to shake. A reputation that preceded us—literally existed before the Lab School—and which fed off any and every misstep or perceived misstep that we took. Every time a Lab School student was out of line, we became, in the minds of some, "those alternative school misfits." Every time we went on a field trip it was "that flaky alternative school that avoids real academic work." Every time word got out about something in community meeting it was "those kids run the school" and every time one of our students was implicated (for good reason or not) in a drug or alcohol situation it was "druggie Lab School."

At fifteen weeks we held our next round of oral presentations. We got the kids going on their research sooner this time, gave more guidance, and indicated that their research this time around would form the basis of research for the twenty-week presentations. On the whole, we were pleased to see improvement. Fewer kids choked, and a few really excelled. One memorable presentation came from Alexi Pinzel, a spunky, bright, and hardworking sophomore who decided to study the effect of European diseases on the Native American population. Her research included a good sampling of secondary sources but, not satisfied with what she had found there, Alexi called the Bureau of Indian Affairs in Washington. Alexi was referred to an M.D. who had conducted original research into the subject and might be willing to share his findings. Alexi continued to follow through and in the end included in her report excerpts from her phone interview with the doctor. Together with her other sources and a lucid presentation, including well-designed tables, Alexi delivered a real tour de force, a model for other kids. The audience (her Lab School peers) was still during Alexi's presentation, struck dumb by the indisputable authority with which she spoke and carried herself. *My god*, they must have thought, *no way could I do that*, or, maybe, *she's gonna make us all look bad*, or maybe *way to go, Alexi*. It was probably all of those. In my mind it was, Why can't they all do this? And, they can do this, all of them. They are capable. Thank you, Alexi.

We had invited our high school colleagues to observe the fifteen-week presentations, having posted a note on the door in the faculty room and made a general invitation during the last faculty meeting for all who were available to join us, even if only for one presentation. Only two showed up. There was still a fair amount of standoffishness about Lab School among the faculty. And, at a much more practical level, it is so very difficult to find the time as a teacher for anything beyond one's immediate responsibilities, that there is just no time to observe the innovations of colleagues.

There is a deep cynicism trimmed out with bitterness in the teaching profession. It affects all of us to a greater or lesser extent. It is cynicism about kids and bitterness about a social tendency to blame teachers for the failure of kids in school. We end up taking the rap for too much TV, not enough parental attention, too much instant gratification, too little character development, too much character development, when there are other social forces that are more responsible for all these pathologies.

Yes, it is true. Kids have a shorter attention span than they did a generation ago—and all the rest—but what we in teaching sometimes fail to acknowledge is that we use all those social failures to excuse our own professional shortcomings. If we fail to inspire our students is society wholly to blame? If our kids roll over and play dead academically, does that mean it's okay for us to stop caring? Yes, it is probably more challenging to be a public school teacher right now than it has been ever in the history of American public education, but the basic formula for being a successful teacher has not changed: show kids you care, offer them trust, responsibility, and privilege in ways that are appropriate to their age, expect much of them academically, and strive for creative, intellectually respectful ways of engaging their minds—with humor and play but never frivolously, for school must be hard work and must be viewed that way by students. Between the bonds of mutual support and communication we were building with our students and were establishing with their parents, the Lab School was starting to get it right.

"When I got that letter, I felt like I'd just gotten a final disconnect notice from the power company." Mrs. Berkowitz looked me square in the eye. The fish tank bubbled resolutely in the corner of Jane's science classroom. Late afternoon sunlight, weakened and diffused by winter cloud cover, filtered into the room through venetian blinds. Our circle of student desks was drawn close: Mr. and Mrs. Berkowitz, Donny, the guidance counselor, and the teachers. The letter was one of twenty-two that we mailed home shortly after second-quarter grades went out. The parents of any student whose progress suggested that he or she might not graduate on time received this letter. There were twenty-two letters and we had fifty-four students in the program. We were betting the ranch.

Jane jumped into the silence. "Why don't we take a minute to hear from each of Donny's teachers to see where we stand." This seemed reasonable. I began.

"Well, of seven topics covered so far in humanities during the

99

first semester, Donny has mastered with a grade of "4" only two of them." I added that Donny was capable of doing better and just needed to apply himself.

Mrs. Berkowitz replied without skipping a beat that Donny *was* working. He was working harder than she had ever known him work.

"Then it will come," I answered, trying to muster a tone of knowing confidence. The other teachers spoke. Same thing. Marginal grades, needs to work harder. We talked about time management and study skills, and then, somewhat spontaneously we started talking about something we hadn't previously discussed in a family conference: about how many high school students waltz through high school, coddled by the system, raising marginal grades to passing by last-minute effort or just drifting along content with a gentleman's B, but then facing a crisis when they get to college: seminars where there are no daily homework assignments to buoy up a poor exam grade, lecture courses where the professor has no idea who you are, and that winning disposition you've cultivated won't even register in the professor's calculation of your grade because he doesn't know your name. Courses where maybe one paper and two tests determine your entire grade and you can't wait until the night before and expect to do it all well. Because of the way Lab School is set up, we offered, Donny was facing that crisis now. We then delivered the punch line: isn't it better for him to face this now within the supportive environment of the Lab School rather than the first semester of his freshman year at college with no support network?

It had the ring of truth. Mr. and Mrs. Berkowitz and Donny all seemed to hunker down at this point in the conversation with a slowly gathering determination that this was Donny's moment of truth. Yes, he could bail out of this program but maybe that would just be a cop-out. Why not tackle this thing now so Donny can really begin to excel?

I could nearly hear them thinking, *These teachers are right, dear.* And Donny. Part of Donny was saying, *I'm licked.* The other part of Donny was uttering with resignation, *Time to grow up.*

During late February and March after the famous letter, we held a score of family conferences. We were averaging three to four a week, sometimes running to an hour and a half each, a grueling pace on top of everything else. Everything else. We'd hit a crucial point in our development, a defining moment for our fledgling program. Our continued existence hung in the balance. On the one hand, we needed parent support in order to give us credibility and help bring new students on board. On the other hand, the Lab School had to live up to its alleged standard of excellence. We could not forsake our standards, we had determined months before, even if it meant the death of the program. And maybe it would. There were calls of concern from parents coming into the central administration offices, expressions of doubt as to where this program was headed. Our sign-ups for the next school year, completed in February, were low. We wanted thirty-three incoming sophomores, but the numbers seemed to be in the twenties. Word was starting to circulate that some families were seriously planning to bail out. Robert Bojet, it seemed, wanted out. When, during a family conference in February, we suggested it would really be a bad move and tried with everything in our persuasive arsenal to hold him to his commitment to the program, Mom and Dad reacted and began calling administrators, school board members, the state education department, and Lab School parents, insisting that Robert get out. Now. Immediately.

What to do.

There were three main strands of concern, rising and fraying all at the same time: one, sign ups were low for the coming year; two, some families were losing faith; and, three, a few families were taking steps toward the door. The sign-up situation had been evolving since December and was a source of great frustration because initially there seemed to be a great deal of interest in Lab School among the freshmen but somehow it had gotten snuffed out. Our promotional campaign for the next year's sign ups began in December and had followed pretty much the same course as the previous year. First, a letter of invitation went home to all parents of ninth graders. This was followed within a couple of days by an in-school presentation for all ninth-grade students. The previous year, the in-school presentation had consisted of an overhead projector and me. This year, now that we had real live Lab School students, it became infinitely more animated. After an introduction led by the teachers, we had our students lead small discussion groups with the ninth graders. Rotating through ninth-grade English classes, we covered all the freshmen in two days. One English teacher, eavesdropping on discussion groups, reported that the message going to freshmen was generally, "We work hard but we like it." Couldn't ask for a better testimony. That was it. That's what we were after. Based on a survey taken after each session, nearly 140 ninth graders were interested in the program. We felt buoyant, and all went home for Christmas break. As with the previous year, we calculated that the combination of the in-school presentation and letter to parents would stimulate some conversation at home during the holidays. We therefore planned an evening meeting at school for the week after the holiday break for all interested parents.

It snowed. The afternoon of the event, a snow advisory was declared and by seven P.M., three inches lay on the ground with still more swirling earthward. We decided in the afternoon that the show must go on since, if we canceled, there would surely be some people showing up anyway and if all they found was a locked door, they just might say harumph to Lab School and never come back.

So we held it, complete with panel discussion. We had assembled a group of current students and parents to answer questions after our teacher intro. About sixty people showed (good thing we held it), and the meeting went extremely well. Our parents, in particular, really came through for us. They were indeed, effusive, exclaiming that their children were working harder than they'd ever seen: writing more, doing more homework, caring about their studies. If it was parent testimonials that our potential customers wanted to hear, they got it that night. We left the meeting optimistic about how it had gone, but concerned about the numbers. If the pool of potential enrollees was represented by these sixty people, some of whom were couples, just how many sign-ups would there actually be?

We held a makeup session the following week. Evening two brought about twenty-five people. We grew concerned. What if nobody signed up? Would we be allowed to continue the next year? What would the psychological cost be to our current students? We spoke with the guidance counselors and, based on preliminary course sign-ups, the estimate ranged from a low of nine to a high of twenty-seven. I began to feel that same stomach churning anxiety I had endured the previous February during course sign-ups. I determined that I would not allow myself to ride that same emotional roller coaster.

Once we felt we had done all we could for sign-ups (which turned out to be not much), we turned our attention back to student progress. It was at this point, around mid-February that, upon reviewing our students' grades, we realized that something drastic needed to be done. A message, strong and clear, needed to be sent to some students—let's say an alarmingly large minority—that they were not getting their work done, and that if they didn't start doing their work they would in all likelihood find themselves spending an additional semester or year in Lab School. So that's what we did. The letter went out to the parents of those twenty-two students. It was Michele who spoke most vehemently that the letter needed to go out, and it was she who penned it, characteristically direct. Had I written it, the flashing red light message would no doubt have been obscured. Michele laid it on the line. We found ourselves assailed not only by the prospect of low sign-ups but now the added stress of intense family conferences three times a week, plus phone calls, plus lengthy discussion in community meeting. Why, we asked ourselves, do we do this? And, moreover, how were we going to get ourselves through all these self-imposed disasters with both our dignity and our program intact? What to do.

Hold a spaghetti dinner. Like the cavalry, Mrs. Kosinski and Mrs. Ballinger appeared at our door one afternoon at the end of a family conference that had nearly erupted into a fist fight and declared that it was time for the Lab School to hold a spaghetti dinner. A what? It will pull everybody together and raise some money for field trips and computer parts. Great idea, who will organize it? We will, said Mrs. Kosinski and Mrs. Ballinger. Angels of mercy.

The introduction of their idea was a spark that ignited a little flame that grew eventually into a warming fire that, indeed, pulled the Lab School back together. The next day, we decided it was time to plan another Lab School breakfast. We needed to address all these concerns squarely and collectively. We scheduled the breakfast for two weeks hence, and learning from the first breakfast, decided not to hold it theater style with all the teachers down front. Instead, we invited parents to join with the students in their advisory groups for general discussion during the first period. Then we would meet together in room 46 where the advisory groups would report their highlights. Les Loomis, Judy Wooster, and Jon Hunter all agreed to come, too, knowing full well it could be a rough ride. As it turned out, what could have been a very negative, sour, and polemical debate, turned into a constructive, frank, and very useful discussion. Reasoned minds prevailed and, again, we took good notes. The number one concern was with the report card format; not the course work or grades. Indeed, there was no suggestion that our standards were too high (amazingly, despite the twenty-two letters); rather, the concern was with the reporting of the first four goals. They seemed arbitrary, ill-defined, and reading between the lines, maybe presumptuous. Another concern, surfacing in less direct ways, wasn't really a concern; it was a modest feeling of disappointment that our students were not being allowed to express their personal interest in academic ways. We had promised a program that would seek that elusive point of intersection between the natural interests that kids have and worthy academic goals, yet we were failing to deliver.

Part of me wanted page one of the report to just go away. It was extremely time consuming to complete, widely misunderstood by students and parents, and now the cause of ill will. Why bother! On the other hand, page one made us unique as a school. Page one identified graduation goals that were consummately worthy but generally ignored by public schools: adept thinker and problem solver; confident and mature individual, etc. We couldn't and wouldn't want to just chuck all that. It occurred to me at some point in our ruminations on this subject that, two years prior, one of the design team subgroups had devised a scheme (which we ultimately rejected) that had kids simultaneously conducting traditional course work in the usual way and special-interest projects of their own design on a contract basis. What if we retained page one as is, but instead of posting grades there based on course work, students would complete projects of their own design based on outside interests. Goals that the project would satisfy would be determined in advance and scored upon completion. On the report card, only scores for those goal areas where a project had been completed would be posted. If a student had not yet completed a project in a certain goal area, that goal would be unscored on the report card. Over the course of a student's Lab School experience, she would be responsible to see that something was completed satisfactorily (4 or better) for each goal area so that by graduation, all goals would be met.

The team, as eager as I for a solution to this problem, fairly quickly accepted the concept. Jane expressed concern that there would no longer be a way to indicate progress with skills in the academic courses. Good point. So we appended a short list of academic skills to page two with a label indicating that scores there were based on performance in the academic classes. Next, we put together a package describing the new "portfolio projects" with guidelines for the "contract" and we were ready to put it in place.

But wait a minute—we checked ourselves. For a change of this magnitude, shouldn't we run it by our clients for a preview and further input? We could not afford another false start. If we were going to make changes in response to parent concerns we'd better make sure the changes were going to fix the problems targeted as well as avoid creating new problems. To that end, we scheduled an evening "workshop" with parents to review modifications in the report card. It was a gesture of good faith really. We wanted to make clear to parents in a substantial way that we cared about their concerns and we were listening. The meeting was scheduled for the Lab School room and the chairs arranged in a big circle. Also on the agenda was a discussion of delayed graduation. Our most recent edition of FUTURES had quite directly raised three issues: report card revision, the specter of delayed graduation, and the untenable workload faced by our teachers. Those three issues were the agenda.

About fifty people showed up. All parents. (We had indicated that we wanted this to be for parents only.) There were nods of general approval to the suggested report card revisions. We seemed to be on the money there. We turned then to the issue of delayed graduation, saying how the Lab School is a mastery-based program necessitating some variation as to when students might graduate. Here, mixed responses form the audience.

It is a great contradiction really that while society recognizes that children learn at different rates, it expects them all to graduate from high school at the same time, indeed, on the very same day. And the importance of graduating on time is not trivial. So much is tied to it: the launching of a college career, all the rituals attendant to graduation, and an abiding identification with the class of ———. Accepting variation in the graduation date from student to student is far more than a logistical problem, it is a matter of changing a firmly entrenched culture.

Given the expectation for on-time graduation, our discussion at the parent workshop was actually quite open. While some parents stated with mild defiance they didn't know delayed graduation was a possibility when they signed up for Lab School, others were showing some openness to the idea. Paul Ireland: "I am one of the parents who received that letter saying my son might not graduate on time, and I think that might be a good thing. I'm more interested in seeing William graduate when he's ready and really knows what he needs to, even if it means he's got to take an extra year to get it right."

Josh Nailor's father: "What we're talking about is changing a culture. We have to stop thinking in terms of the class of so and so, and sophomores and seniors, and all that. We have to think in terms of mastery."

The last item on the agenda (teacher burnout) we never got to, partly because time ran out but partly, I think, because we felt awkward about discussing it. That parents had been alerted to it was perhaps enough. To discuss it further might have been seen by some as indulgent.

The workshop helped. A lot. Through the grapevine in the following weeks word was that the parents were impressed that we presented them with "drafts" and "proposals" before we adopted new policies. Meanwhile, though, we were facing a new front in community meeting. Since September, we had been faithfully holding our community meetings every week addressing issues and so forth. But there was a growing frustration on the part of students that issues were not being resolved, that discussions would ramble on without any real resolution, and that next week's meeting would pick up on new business without going back and closing out the old business from last week's meeting. In short, the kids were beginning to feel that community meeting was a sham. At a meeting in February, they confronted us with this and as the discussion proceeded, someone, a student, suggested that a committee be formed to revamp community meeting. And so it was. And so they did. The next week Paul Inkfuss presented a proposal from the committee. The proposal established a permanent agenda committee to be composed of two members from each advisory group. The agenda committee would solicit agenda items from classmates during advisory group each week. Then they would be excused fifteen minutes early from advisory to meet together and form an agenda for community meeting the next day. The chair of community meeting would come from the agenda committee and the responsibility would rotate. Furthermore, the proposal offered that the disposition of each agenda item would be tracked and that before closing the discussion on an item it would be formally tabled, referred to committee, or resolved. With only brief discussion about how many students should serve on the agenda committee and for how long, the proposal was adopted by consensus.

At the next community meeting the new process was set in motion. From the first of the revised meetings, the students appeared considerably more enthusiastic, wasting no time to get the meeting underway, leading it themselves, and tracking progress in a "Lab School Notebook."

One of the first issues to be discussed under the new arrangement had to do with remediation, and it was brought by the teachers. We were growing more and more concerned about students not turning in work on time. It was not uncommon for less than half the class to submit an assignment on the date due. Why was this happening? Mainly, we determined, because of abuse of our mastery-based system. It was our policy to allow students to redo an assignment as many times as they reasonably could until they had achieved at least a grade of four. Unfortunately, some students took this to mean they could delay submitting assignments until the end of the quarter, which created all kind of problems. First, it meant they were not keeping up with the class, which would have proceeded through lessons X, Y, and Z before they had begun lesson A; second it meant that the teachers were getting buried in late work the last week of the quarter. Third and most importantly, the concept of mastery was being thwarted.

So we raised the issue at community meeting and faced some stiff resistance. Abusers of the system could not argue persuasively but there were some students, mostly responsible ones who turned in their work on time, who argued that we shouldn't change the system and that students should not be penalized for late work for the simple reason that they were only hurting themselves by abusing the system. Imposing a penalty, especially a grade penalty, would philosophically go against the whole notion of mastery, they said, which confers credit when mastery is achieved regardless of when mastery occurs.

They were, unfortunately, quite eloquent, and we did not know how to respond with equal persuasiveness. Try as we may, they pretty much carried the argument. But the issue remained unresolved, so a committee was formed to look into it. The remediation committee met and reported to community meeting two weeks later. Their proposal was a compromise. They invoked a minor grade penalty for late submission along with guidelines to better manage the time students were allowed to remediate work already submitted. After protracted discussion in which the holdouts tried to insist on no penalty at all for late work, we finally reached consensus. The holdouts agreed to adopt the scheme on a trial basis. We were hopeful but feared the abusers would still abuse as the sanctions against late submission were not very serious.

Were the holdouts right? Yes and no. Yes in that mastery meant mastery regardless of when it was attained. No, in that tardiness is a separate issue. A student who continuously tries ought to be encouraged until he achieves mastery. A student who delays making any effort until the last minute ought to be penalized. The key, as we would later determine would be to make the penalty something other than academic. But we had to endure one more semester of widespread abuse before coming to this simple realization.

Meanwhile, the Robert Bojet situation wasn't going away. Robert and family were seriously considering quitting the program. We were in a real quandary over this one as there were several issues at stake. First, we wanted our policy discouraging transfers to be meaningful. At the same time, we agreed, it should not and could not be ironclad. When policies become ironclad, institutions cease being human and become machines. There always needs to be room for judgment to override policy. This was not such a case, though. Our judgment was squarely aligned with the policy. There was no good reason for Robert to transfer out. But then the question was, Should we stand fast on principle knowing that doing so would consume a great deal of time? We needed that time to spend working with students and developing the program. In addition it would probably generate a good deal of ill will and grist for the rumor mill that we would then have to spend additional time (which we did not have) correcting. The third and most important issue was whether in the end it would serve Robert's best interest to remain in the program when both he and his parents so adamantly wanted out. In the end, we relented. It was inevitable. We are a public school after all. Personally, I wish we had pushed the issue a little harder just to make it clear to the Bojets (and all who through the grapevine were following the saga) that the Lab School stood for decent standards and that as professionals we would not endorse mediocrity—we might have to accept it in matters not entirely under our control, but we would not endorse it. I hope that in whatever path Robert's life has since followed, he has determined to apply himself and accept nothing less than his best effort.

8

February and March had been the nadir of our first year. The time of year—postholiday season, prespring, winter lingering interminably on—played a role. But, for the most part, internal events had worn us down. Shortly, however, things began to turn around. Mrs. Kosinski and Mrs. Bollinger were beating the spaghetti dinner drum steadily. At the second breakfast, they had introduced the idea, polled the crowd on dates, and passed around a list for committee sign ups. By early March, their committees were organized and busy at work. And they were doing it all. The teachers were asked to do very little. There seemed to be a tacit understanding that it would be that way, a kind of gift of contributed services by the parents as if to say thank you for all the time and effort the teachers were putting in. Our only contributions were to attend a meeting each, pass out forms in class, and sign up students for services (child care, lawn mowing, etc.) to be auctioned off at the dinner. There was an esprit de corps that emerged from the planning and committee work, and it grew from and among the parents.

113

About that time, too, the student newspaper at the high school decided to do a story on the Lab School. Naturally, this made us nervous. With all the challenges we'd been facing, the last thing we wanted was a story describing our trials and tribulations to the community. But one cannot impede the press. Their reporter decided to conduct a survey and asked us to administer it in class. Fair enough. The survey asked good, direct questions, the kind you tell yourself you shouldn't be afraid of but nevertheless are: (1) Are you learning more at the Lab School than you did last year? (2) Is the schedule at the Lab School more conducive to learning? (3) Does the Lab School still have problems to be worked out? (4) If you were a freshman again, would you sign up for the Lab School? We held our breath and awaited the results, which arrived via the reporter, who now wanted to interview me. Answer to question one: 45 yes, 1 no; question two: 42 yes, 2 no; question three: 43 yes, 2 no; question four: 44 yes, 4 no. I was elated, but on my guard as the reporter began to ask how I would interpret the results. Is Lab School better than high school? *For some. I don't believe in cookie-cutter schools. Families should be able to choose from among different school programs the one that best suits their child's needs and personality.* Will the whole high school eventually be set up like the Lab School? *That's not for me to say, but it's important to remember that the teachers and the kids volunteered to do the Lab School. If everybody was forced into it, you'd have a completely different program.*

That night, we were able to open the parent workshop with the good news. The relief was visible. Finally, we got a break! Much of the anxiety felt by our parents came from the misconceptions of Lab School that they were constantly faced with around town. Your daughter might be having fun but is she learning anything? Isn't that where all the teachers send their misfits? That's the druggie school. Positive PR was as welcome as rain to parched earth. But there was a troublesome side to the good news as well. Word began to circulate that the newspaper's survey results (yet to be published) would be out with the next issue along with an accompanying story that was rumored to be very positive. An administrator took me aside several days after the parent meeting and in the course of our conversation suggested that if I could influence the reporter at all I might try to tone down the article a little—for political reasons.

About this time, there was some more potentially good news percolating in another area. A month before, I'd gotten a call from Dardis McNamee, a well-known journalist in the area, who said she'd heard about the Lab School and was interested in doing a story "on speculation" for a major publication. She had my attention. Could she come by tomorrow? Ah, sure. Journalists always want the interview yesterday. Her timing was good, though, and she appeared on the second day of midyear exams, pen and reporter's notebook in hand, to observe. Dardis made me nervous; raised in elite private schools, an Ivy League college education. Would she measure our little public school against her halcyon recollection of boarding-school standards or would she see what we were trying desperately to do with a diverse group of public school kids? Our initial phone conversation had been upbeat but now, as I glanced at her across the examining room, she peered skeptically and intently at the scene before her. She interviewed students between presentations. I wondered.

We spoke afterward. "What you're doing here is impressive," she said. "You're attempting, really, to create a classical education within a public school. You're getting the kids to do the thinking while you take on the role of tutor or coach, giving guidance from the sidelines."

Hallelujah. Dardis returned several days later to observe regular classes. We were discussing the exams in humanities class, conducting the "postmortem" in Dardis' words. After school we spoke at length. She understood what we were trying to do, and over the next several weeks conducted extensive interviews with parents and school administrators. I had given her a list of parents and examiners she might speak with, and being a good journalist, she made sure to call parents and examiners not on the list as well. In the end, she produced a substantial, in-depth article that raved about the program. She called me shortly before it came out to say she could scarcely believe the support and respect Lab School parents had for the program. "You're on to something," she said.

The article appeared in the spring issue of *Innovating* a professional journal targeted mainly to social service agencies and academia. The article reprints have been most beneficial for Lab School inquiries.

Our star, out of orbit and hurtling earthward in February, was rising. Kosinski and Ballinger were moving rapidly toward Pasta Dinner D-Day. (The publicity committee had adopted "pasta" as more upscale than "spaghetti" to help justify our ambitious $6 tickets.) They had, in addition to publicity committee, a serving committee, purchasing committee, decorations committee, dessert committee, supplies committee, preparation committee, clean-up committee, auction committee, and a tickets committee. It was all moving along nicely but, as the day approached, ticket sales seemed low—less than two hundred just two days before the event. Our target for profits had been a thousand dollars but, with expenses running around four hundred dollars, that was looking unlikely. We forged ahead. Erin Delaney's grandfather had already made all the sauce and meatballs (twelve hundred) while Jared Nailor's mother had gotten some fifty local merchants to donate all kinds of door prizes.

D-day arrived, ticket holders arrived, and gradually others, too.

The kitchen crew and the servers swung into action. Then more people, and we added servers. Then more people, and we set additional tables. They kept coming, a steady stream all through the dinner hour. In the end, we served up three hundred fifty dinners. Combined with proceeds from the auction of student services, we cleared eighteen hundred dollars after expenses.

March and April were fast becoming our season of success. With the favorable press and good spirits generated by the pasta dinner, things were looking up. A photographer from the local paper who had been snapping away at the dinner got a shot of my daughter and me hamming it up with our pasta. Next week we were plastered on the front page over the banner "Pasta Perfect." A full page of candids from the dinner filled the newspaper's centerfold. Great coverage—and trouble. Whenever Lab School drew attention to itself, it raised the ire of certain colleagues.

In the week after our pasta madness, a meeting of the impact group was called to address "some issues." The members of the impact group were good people, some, former members of the Lab School design team. But in their role as impact group, they had to represent all factions, which indeed they did.

"There is some concern," we were informed as we all assembled in the principal's office, "that holding a fund-raiser like the pasta dinner sets a precedent."

A precedent for what?

"Well, if we're able to pay for necessities like computers and books and microscopes through fund-raisers, the Board of Education might deny future requests for equipment and suggest that we hold a fund raiser—like the Lab School did."

"There is concern also," we were told, "about numbers—student-to-staff ratio." Our staffing had been set in March at 3.6 FTE based on a projected enrollment of seventy students. Apparently, to some, this was already a rich ratio. What if some kids dropped, as seemed quite possible ("likely" as some of our not so supportive colleagues happily chirped). Was there a mechanism to return staffing to the high school and at what point would it be employed?

On the one hand, it is frustrating to be roaring ahead with an exciting new program and all the while have antagonists at your heels. On the other hand, distrust of district decision making was rooted in a long history of contentiousness between the two sides. The impact group was only doing its job, seeing that all matters regarding the Lab School were fair and aboveboard. But we were stuck in the middle.

The Lab School's first year may be likened to starting a small business in a communist country like East Germany—back when it was East Germany. So much of what we were trying to do was just plain alien to the system: marketing, promotion, pizzazz. You paint the canopy over your storefront a bright color and the workers at the government-run store next door complain that you are attracting customers. You put out a few extra display cases and the local party leader says you're making the other workers look bad. You make a special effort to keep your customers happy and you are accused of setting a precedent of extra work that other shopkeepers will have to follow. The pressure to toe the line, to fall back into the accustomed modes of behavior, is great. It's a lot easier to adopt universal beige as your color. It's a lot harder to resist. Public education does not roll out the red carpet for entrepreneurs. It tries mightily to expel them like an invading virus that could wipe out the system. To stay the course is very hard.

We left the impact meeting angry. We felt caught in a hopelessly entrenched system in which no individual or constituency is to blame, but the entire system is at fault. The image that comes to mind is a pointillist painting, only the effect is reversed. Up close, Seurat is just a mass of dots, but as you step back the dots form patterns and patterns become a picture. Public education is sort of the opposite: when you look at all the parts up close, they make sense. The union makes sense when they talk about fearful precedents. The board makes sense when they talk about union paranoia, the administrators make sense when they talk about a quest for excellence, and we make sense (I hope) when we talk about the need for innovation in schools. But if you step back and look at the whole thing, it makes no sense at all. All you see is dots, beige dots.

The pasta dinner had done the trick as far as rekindling team spirit. Winter weather, relentless through March, was giving way to warmer days. The snow piles ringing the school parking lots were turning black, small, and old, and we had a big field trip planned to Ellis Island and the Statue of Liberty. The trip turned out to be a great success except that three of our young scholars decided to exercise their liberties by smoking a joint and got caught by federal marshals.

One of the great hypocrisies of American society lies in its attitudes toward drugs and alcohol. Nowhere is this hypocrisy more pointed than in its application to teenagers. Our public laws and social attitudes defy basic psychology and common sense. Underage drinking concerns us so we raise the age, increasing both the allure of alcohol to young people as well as the total potential number of underage drinkers. Marijuana gets us spooked, so we generate a lot of lopsided scientific evidence for its hazardous aspects only, expecting naively that teenagers will get scared away. Meanwhile, of course, the adult public drinks merrily and celebrates its collective habit regularly in the media. I can think of no better formula than that constituted by our current laws and attitudes to promote reckless use of alcohol and drugs by young people.

It should come as no surprise then when kids do something so flagrant as to smoke a joint openly on federal property while on a school field trip. Thus were we summoned into the park ranger's office where our three lads were being held in custody. Rights were read, chemical tests performed, parents and school officials called, releases signed, and a general pall fell upon the day. All the kids, of course, knew about the arrest a good half an hour before any of the adults who were attempting to track down the missing youths.

Next day, the faculty room was abuzz. No doubt the grapevine had already reached out to the community also. The dilemma for us was shaping up like this. On the one hand, we had a responsibility to look after the welfare of the students involved, at least one of whom we suspected of having a dangerous dependence on drugs already. We also felt a responsibility to inform all our parents of the incident out of respect for their rights to know what goes on in their children's school, for good or ill. On the other hand, sharing all this information would mean providing the rumor mill with enough grist to feed a whole bellyful of scandal mongers.

We stiffened our backs and did what we had to do. The next issue of *Futures* carried a notice of the event and we held an evening meeting the following week, which focused mainly on drugs and alcohol. The rumor mill got a bellyful and we maintained our integrity. The kids? The event stimulated much discussion and, I hope, a heightened sensitivity. An interesting and ironic footnote to the whole episode is that the morning of that same field trip, one of our students was pulled over by the local constabulary for speeding in a school zone and issued a ticket (an ill-fated predeparture bagel run). This became the target of much jesting both during and after the trip. During a student discussion about the marijuana episode, one classmate stated how unfair it was that the traffic violation earned a greater penalty (fine, suspension of license) than the "much more serious" marijuana incident ($50 fine). Am I alone in observing an irony in both the student's comment and the lighthearted attitude of the students generally toward the traffic violation? It seems to me that speeding in a school zone, which poses an imminent threat to life, is at least as serious as smoking a joint. Apparently our pseudo-temperance views have effected some kooky values in some of our kids.

Meanwhile, another issue was heating up involving one of our classrooms. One of the rooms that we had been using was in demand by other teachers for next year. And the assertiveness with which certain members of the affected department were laying claim to the space for the coming year was upsetting. Despite the fact that we were making fuller use of the space, including two adjacent prep rooms, than had been made in years, our argument, based on the relative merits of program need were overwhelmed by issues of turf and ego. After several faculty discussions turned into unpleasant exchanges, we decided it would be better to take the less suitable space we were being offered and avoid further tension. Overall, faculty relations were a growing concern. While most teachers either quietly supported us, were neutral, or were open in their skepticism, there was a significant minority that seemed threatened by our presence. Why remains a mystery. Perhaps it was the criticism of conventional education that the establishment of the Lab School implied. Why do we need a Lab School unless there's something wrong with things as they are? Second was perhaps a more personal issue: some colleagues had toiled for years quietly building excellent programs and had never won public recognition for their efforts. Now along came the Lab School and not even a year into implementation its glories were being heralded. There might understandably be some hurt feelings (to which we needed to be sensitive). Third was a fear that all this Lab School stuff was a wedge into the resolve of some teachers that the school programs were fine and what needed changing was student and parent attitudes that had eroded considerably since the "golden age" (some variously defined earlier time). Moreover, it was a fear that the "Lab School way," voluntary during the first years, would be eventually imposed on all by decree, and, like every other education fad during the last thirty years, would hobble the good work of schools until the next fad came along.

Competition, ambition, entrepreneurship, child advocacy—all are alien to at least some parts of our system of public education. And while individuals may deny it and while others may strive against it, the overwhelming characteristic of the system is faceless, bureaucratic, lumbering, and foolish—a warehousing system for America's youth that stifles personality, spirit, community, and stunts our country's future.

Around this time we began work in earnest on a waiver application. New York State had recently adopted "The New Compact for Learning," Education Commissioner Thomas Sobol's initiative to give local school's greater autonomy on the assumption that autonomy is crucial to institutional excellence (right assumption). One major step in implementing the new compact was soliciting proposals from public schools for innovative programs. If the proposals met guidelines established by the Education Department, then the department would waive appropriate regulations so that the school could offer a Regents diploma to its graduates. Our Lab School, which drew some inspiration from Sobol's pronouncements, had so far made no real effort to seek a waiver. We had been on the fence about the whole process since the days of the design team. On the one hand, we felt little urgency about seeking "Regents" certification since most colleges place little or no value on it. And since we were trying to break free of the regents strictures it seemed counterproductive to pursue it. On the other hand, countless parents had either stated or implied that they would enroll their children in Lab School except for the lack of a regents diploma. Bethlehem serves as a bedroom community for many state workers, some of whom work for the State Education Department, people who had been writing regents course syllabi and regents exams for years. Traditional expectations in our town were unusually high. And, after all, the waiver process that had been set up was intended not to bend innovation to the regents' will, but rather to bless worthy grassroots projects with an official state-level affirmation. Of course, the real reason we had not as yet pursued it was that we didn't have time.

In the spring of our first year, desire and opportunity finally met and we began the application process. Judy Wooster spearheaded the effort and found that in addition to carefully filling out all the paperwork, making phone contact with the department was also helpful in moving our application along. The department, no doubt, was fearful about opening the waiver floodgate because if all these "innovative authentic, grassroots" programs were endorsed and then turned out to be mickey mouse, it is the department that would take the blame. The state officials needed to feel they could trust these programs. What better way to build trust in the program than to establish trust with the people carrying it out. Judy was smart.

My fear in petitioning the great education behemoth was that it would not speak our language. The language of the department grew out of the bureaucratic social science culture that suffuses the education establishment generally, the chief assumptions of which are centralized authority and scientific rationality. I remember a discussion with one Education Department official a couple of years earlier, a good man, a thinker, but a career bureaucrat. We were arguing about the regents exams. He was complaining that Sobol's effort to break up the exam system would lead to the demise of standards. I questioned why he should assume that the Education Departments' standard would be higher than whatever teachers out there in the hinterland might establish on their own. But... but... but what about accountability, oversight, control? They're all still there, I argued, only it's different people and different forces exercising them.

This is the dominant bureaucratic attitude in the department held in a "but, of course" sort of way—who would ever question it? It is a most basic assumption, the traditional raison d'être of the institution. Coupled with it is a social scientific way of looking at the process of education—something that uses words like *validity, reliability, standard deviation, control group, objectives, generalizability,* and *needs assessment*—as though the practice of teaching were a scientific laboratory experiment, a purely rational activity. I suppose good laboratory scientists don't even view their work this way any more. But doctors of education in their quest to appear as legitimate as their counterpart doctors in the social and physical sciences profess a faith in reason and the Newtonian universe more ardently than the colleagues they seek to emulate (who are presently abandoning the Newtonian world view). If I were asked about the reliability and validity of the Board of Examiners it would simply be the wrong question, just as if I asked the head of the testing bureau if the regents exam in U.S. history is meaningful. Wrong question. We come from very different points of view. The language we use involves words like *meaning* and *value* (not "values"), *passion, inspiration, excellence, expertise, mastery, judgment, reputation, growth, maturity, honor, nurturing, trust,* and so on. How does a top-notch prep school ensure reliability and validity? Not by submitting to educationist bean counters with social scientific micrometers. Rather, by placing their reputation at stake. If their graduates "can't do," the reputation of the institution and its faculty suffers. Fewer students apply, well-qualified faculty leave, the place falls apart.

This is all to say I feared a clash of worldviews from which I would walk away morally vindicated and empty handed (no regents waiver). I believe that the commissioner and the regents (who hired him) understood this more humanistic worldview and subscribed to it, but we would not be dealing with them. We would be dealing with the Ed.D.s and bureau associates, some of whom were quite at odds with their relatively new and not especially well liked commander in chief. Could we make them understand? Could we beat the system by going through it? An odd construction.

# 9

"But, what do you *think* about it, Tanya?"

"I don't think about it, Mr. Nehring. I mean, I have an opinion, but like it doesn't matter 'cause like you have an opinion, too. Everybody's opinion is different. It's cool."

"So, then, Tanya, what *is* your opinion and why do you hold that opinion?"

"Mr. Nehring, don't you see. It doesn't matter what my opinion is."

This exchange is part of a larger conversation that Tanya and I held during an advisory group session one week in May. We were discussing a controversial plan before the Town Board to switch the town's water source from an area reservoir to a ground water source of debatable purity beneath the Hudson River.

"But, Tanya, it *does* matter what your opinion is because you can influence the decision that will be made about the water you drink in your home."

Somehow, legions of contemporary teenagers have gotten the impression that opinions don't matter and that, therefore, the defensibility of opinions doesn't matter either. I encounter this attitude somewhere between occasionally and frequently among students and have puzzled over it a fair amount. I speculate it draws from three sources. One: teachers, ever cautious not to impose their own opinions on impressionable minds often withhold their opinions from class discussion—a wise caution—which is unintentionally interpreted by some students to mean opinions are something adults don't talk about. Two: teachers, eager to teach their students that no one opinion is ever gospel truth will declare "There is no right answer. Your opinion is as good as the next person's." Again, a virtuous motive is at work, but epistemologically, the construction makes one want to bang one's head against the wall. That there is no "right" answer suggests that we dwell either in a universe of wrong answers or that somehow the rightness of answers is not relevant since apparently it is okay for everyone to disagree or that there is an inherent impotency in the human condition where right answers are unknowable and human action is therefore ineffectual. "Your opinion is as good as mine" suggests, furthermore, that the sapiens part of homo sapiens is a trait of no consequence, since apparently a careless opinion is of equal value with a carefully reasoned opinion. One may draw the town's water supply from beneath the local Mobil gas station as from a pristine mountain lake. It doesn't matter. Three: students who are very subject to the same occasional intellectual laziness that can afflict us all, will excuse a decision to not think by drawing on points one and two above.

That our students think is *the* matter of central importance to all our efforts in school. As our experience with the fifty-odd students in the Lab School increased, the urgency of getting students to think impressed us all. Knowing our Lab School students better than we had ever known students before, we gained a new appreciation for the intellectual docility that seems to characterize teenagers today (maybe always has, only now the stakes are higher). We noticed this especially in the twenty-week projects, and when the forty-week projects got underway we noticed it again. This time, however, I was better prepared. As the forty-week projects got started, I announced that any student choosing a history topic would be required to write a position paper in which a position (thesis, opinion) would be clearly stated up front and then defended. In announcing my new decree to the students, I likened the procedure to a court case, a useful gimmick I'd picked up at a conference. You, I told the students are the prosecuting attorney. Like her you are trying to prove your point. Like an attorney, you make an opening statement: "Ladies and gentlemen of the jury, I will prove to you that . . ." Like an attorney you will then present evidence, witnesses, expert testimony, and documents before your "jury" (the Board of Examiners). You will then close, restating your position summarizing your case, and asserting the inescapable conclusion. The kids seemed to understand it all when I put it in those terms. But still they resisted.

Tanya had begun work on a project dealing with the civil rights movement. Her proposal (which I required of all my students) stated that she would "trace the history of the civil rights movement from the 1950s to the present."

"And what is your position, Tanya?" I asked one day in project block as I was reviewing progress on the forty-week papers.

"I . . . I . . . well, I mean I'm just tracing the history of it is all."

"But you're supposed to be writing a position paper."

"But that's not what I want to do."

"Tanya, let me put it another way. You could go in front of the examiners and "trace" the history of the civil rights movement. You'd mention *Brown v Board of Education,* you'd mention Little Rock, you'd mention the lunch-counter sit-ins, the freedom rides, the march on Washington, I have a dream, the Civil Rights Act of 1964, and all the rest of it. I'm sure it would all be accurate, nicely presented, etc. But you know what? The examiners would sit there and think, so what? We know all this—just like you know it all already, too—this kid hasn't really shown us anything interesting. And they'd probably give you a three at best."

Tanya was listening.

"Now, suppose you went in there and said, "Ladies and gentlemen of the Board of Examiners, I am going to prove to you that the March on Washington of 1963 was actually counterproductive to the civil rights movement; that in fact it hurt the likelihood of passage of the Civil Rights Act by angering southern white congressmen.' And then you parade the evidence: excerpts form the Congressional Record, newspaper accounts from the day, commentary by noted historians. You'd knock their socks off. You'd get at least a 5."

Now Tanya was spooked. She didn't have to say anything. I could tell from her expression that she was completely intimidated. I was asking her to leave the security of a descriptive essay for which she already had all the information she needed, and adopt a different, fearful mode in which she would have to look for things she wasn't certain she could find, interpret material she'd never seen before, and organize it into a coherent argument.

That Tanya and many kids like her are spooked by this sort of assignment shows how little they are accustomed to being challenged in this way, to really think for themselves. When one considers what students read in history (or social studies) classes, it is no wonder that they have a difficult time freeing themselves from a purely descriptive mode. History textbooks are as descriptive as history will allow. They are deliberately purged of as much interpretation, bias, judgment, opinion stating, and so on, as possible. This has two effects, both bad. The textbook ends up giving the impression to a naive mind that it is unbiased and nonjudgmental. This is a dangerous effect since history, no matter how deliberately and thoroughly "cleansed" of bias, is in its nature an enterprise founded on bias, and to create the illusion that there is none is a pernicious seduction. The other ill effect of textbooks is that they suggest to the student rather strongly, by force of example, that the writing of history is a mere chronicling of events without any particular purpose. It is no wonder that Tanya proposed the sort of civil rights paper in which she would "trace the history of events." Tracing events is all she'd ever observed in the way of historical writing.

Thus were we pushing our students, attempting to challenge them to the limits of what they believed themselves capable of (sadly, not much) and, we hoped, well beyond.

Meanwhile, plans were underway for an end-of-the-year overnight conference, an end-of-the-year awards dinner, final year-end report cards, and an assemblage of prominent citizens for our Board of Examiners. I distinctly remember an anxiety dream I had Memorial Day weekend in which I was drowning in multiple responsibilities that had symbolically become an amorphous ooze.

Jane, marvelous Jane, had volunteered to take primary responsibility for both the overnight conference and the awards dinner. Assembling the examiners fell to me. And Michele, kind and patient, who was fast becoming our computer software guru, took on the final report card. Jane was successful in locating a marvelous facility on Lake George for the conference. A former resort now operated by the YMCA, Camp Silver Bay had the amenities of a fancy resort hotel with the prices you'd expect to pay at a YMCA camp. She put together a gala event, three days long with workshops and speakers. Her vision of the event was not as a school field trip, but as a conference. It was a smart idea as it implied an adult event for our students. This was not be a school kids, get-into-mischief, wild, trash-the-hotel, school field trip. It was to be a conference with workshops, speeches, breakout sessions, and the like. The difference was language, but the language would set a tone. At the opening of the conference, Jane planned to have a folder for each student with materials and an individual schedule. She was really going to do it up right.

The awards dinner, too, promised to be a memorable event. We booked a local country club, encouraged students to dress up, and insisted, over scattered protests, on inviting parents. As the planning got underway, an interesting debate evolved in community meeting. Should we give awards (it is an "awards banquet"), and what sort of awards should we give? The kids were divided into two camps on the issue. One argued, yes we should give awards for academic achievement and they should go to a restricted number of students who have done truly outstanding work. After all, they argued, Lab School students tend to not get recognized in the schoolwide award competitions, and when time comes for applying to colleges, they'll need to have a few gold stars to decorate their high school transcript. The other camp argued that the Lab School was not about competition. It was about recognizing the worthy traits that every student possesses and celebrating the accomplishments of all. Selecting out a few students for recognition, they argued, would only breed hostility, breaking down the strong bonds of community. If the former group sounded programmatic, the latter group held a certain moral/idealistic advantage. In the end, it was the first group that won out, probably because the teachers leaned more in their direction. As Jane said at one of the community meetings in late May, "If a student works really hard and achieves in a way that serves as a model for other students, why shouldn't they get an award?" And, she continued, "I would hope that everyone else would congratulate such a student, your classmate, for all the hard work they've done."

Personally, I am divided on the issue. Awards can be an effective motivator but they can also be divisive. The idealists are right, we should celebrate the good qualities in every student. The pragmatists, however, inevitably rule the day because the college admissions game is a serious one.

An interesting secondary debate arose. The suggestion was made that we give out some lighthearted awards, to which everyone quickly assented. But then somebody asked what sort of lighthearted awards, and as the usual categories were rattled off (best couple, most likely to succeed, class clown) some kids started to murmur "count me out." There was, they realized, a certain embarrassment factor built in and some students did not want that. Others argued that some of the "joke" awards might be offensive. Then one student suggested that everyone buddy up with a friend and devise awards for each other. This would ensure awards that were appropriate and nonoffensive. At first, this sounded perfect. But then someone pointed out that distributing (with explanations!) fifty-four individual joke awards plus all the academic awards would keep us out until dawn. Also, someone else pointed out, the meaning and/or humor of the joke awards would undoubtedly be based on private jokes and not widely known circumstances. It was decided, then, that a committee would devise the award categories, the students would vote, and only those who wished to would participate.

This entire decision process, though bordering on comical at times in its grandiloquence, clearly and meaningfully involved the students in some important (to them) decisions, which served two ends: it gave them practical experience in negotiating and reaching decisions, a process they will face continually in their public and private lives, and it gave them power, and having exercised power, they gained a stake in the school. The Lab School became a little bit more their school and that has direct academic pay off. When students feel a part of something, they care and when they care, they work hard.

With the report cards, Michele continued to refine the computer program and began to speak excitedly of a new, more sophisticated system she would devise over the summer that would allow us to more easily enter scores and comments as well as easily manipulate data for various statistical analyses. The Board of Examiners, too, was coming together consisting of a blend of academics and people from the private sector. Also, several members of the Board of Education would again serve.

The end-of-the-year trip to Silver Bay went off extremely well. It was the "conference" Jane had planned it to be. But the awards dinner was the icing on the cake. Almost everybody came—with their parents. And they dressed up. It was the largest gathering of well-dressed high school students in nonrented wear I had ever observed. Thus, in one evening we broke two negative traditions: kids don't want to be seen dead with their parents, and a formal high school banquet requires at least $500 for accouterments and transportation. The spirit of the evening was splendid with speeches, awards, applause, humor, and pride. But what truly made the evening was a gift left silently behind by most of the parents who attended. As we were cleaning up, we gathered a fistful of envelopes that had been left at the head table. It wasn't until two days later, on Sunday afternoon that I finally got around to reading the contents. They were thank-you letters—not just notes and cards—letters, one and two pages long, detailing in moving prose the gratitude parents felt for the positive impact we'd had on their children's lives. They were so moving, I couldn't read them all in one sitting. More than anything else, they helped compensate for the struggle and heartache of launching the Lab School.

It was a good thing we got those letters when we did, because bad news was just arriving on the doorstep. As the final week of the school year got underway, I was summoned to the principal's office. Jon said he wanted to discuss, before it became an issue, something that was definitely going to become an issue. Our numbers were declining. Two students had decided to leave the program, although we urged them not to. They had respected the process of discussing the matter with us, their guidance counselor, and the principal at length before making their final decision. They were out. Also, four ninth graders who initially had signed up had decided now against Lab School. This brought our projected enrollment from seventy to sixty-four. Jon did not need to tell me the implications. If our staffing was not reduced to reflect the declining enrollment, there would be loud protest from some quarters. We tossed around all the different staffing formulas, considered all the options, and, in the end, it looked like two or three of us would have to teach an additional high school class to compensate.

I shared the news first with Jane, the result was crushing coming on the heels of our recent successes. But despair turned quickly to resolve- resolve that we would prove the viability of this program no matter how many stones the world tied around our ankles. Michele took the news well, and she, too, has a natural buoyancy that greatly resists anything that would try to tug her down . She quickly adopted a mood of gritty determination. Neither did Sue despair on hearing the bad news. She has remarkable ability to sail smoothly on an even keel despite the height of the waves and nearness of the rocks. I am struck by the strength of all three of the teachers I was fortunate to work with during our first tumultuous year. They are all fine, strong, competent, imaginative people.

Unusual courage, unusual dedication, unusual imagination. These compliments are unfortunately allies to that small influential circle of cynics. "They can't keep this up forever. They're going to burn out. Nehring is just lucky the Lab School teachers are willing to do all that stuff." And, lurking beneath the surface, "We'd better stop this now before the District expects us all to work this hard."

We are not unusual people. We are capable teachers much like the vast majority of our colleagues. If any of our colleagues was faced with a situation like ours—the opportunity to realize a cherished vision—the inner strength would emerge, and he or she would rise to the challenge. Indeed, we're not the first to launch a new program and we won't be the last. All of us, at different challenging points in our work lives and personal lives, must gather strength and show some grit.

Can we keep it up forever? Strength is not a finite commodity that is slowly or quickly depleted. It is a quality that from moment to moment may burn brightly or die down, depending on circumstances. As long as the fire is stoked, it will burn brightly. Currently, our fire is stoked by the undeniable knowledge that we are making a real difference in the lives of our students. Can any human institution "keep it up" forever? Same answer. Indeed, to seek "forever" and "for everybody" solutions denies the essential dynamism of life. Problems and circumstances are always particular and always changing as are their solutions and resolution. There are no solutions for ever and always. We must continually apply fresh thinking to our lives.

Will the district expect more of everybody because of what we have done in the Lab School? We have neither expanded the workday nor the work year, but we have dedicated ourselves fully within the parameters of our profession's high expectations, as so many of our colleagues do daily. Those few who don't, naturally feel threatened.

The next day, Jane and I were ruminating together. "You know," I said. "If push ever comes to shove, all those great parent letters could really help us out."

"I think we're at shove," said Jane.

Pause.

"What if we wrote a letter directly to the board. Mail it out to each member and just say, look, we're up against the wall. If you believe in this program, then you've got to support us and give us back our staffing. I mean new staffing, not just taken back from the high school."

"And then attach the letters," said Jane.

"And then attach the letters. Right."

We brought Michele on board with our idea but chose, somewhat uneasily, to leave Sue, who was untenured, out of it. We typed up a letter, all signed it, photocopied about twenty of the parent letters (names blacked out), mailed them all out in oversized manila envelopes to each board member and the administrators, and waited.

We didn't have to wait long. The local mail usually reaches its destination the next day. And that day coincidentally found us all (with Sue, who thanked us for not telling her) in Jon's office with the Impact group. We passed around a copy of the letter and hashed over the whole situation for about an hour. The outcome was that we officially lost our staffing. Now we needed to see if the board would be moved to restore it.

To make a long story, involving numerous meetings, shorter, we got our staffing back. Two weeks later at its July public session, the board made it official.

We were elated. In addition to the lightened work load, the action was a clear signal from the board that they believed in what we were doing.

# 10

The Irish elk was a Stone Age native of Europe. The male was known for its large antlers. So large were these antlers that some males raised their heads only with great difficulty. Females, the theory goes, were attracted to large-antlered males and tended to breed with them (as opposed to males with more modest antlers). Thus the big antlers got bigger and bigger over generations to the point where some males couldn't pick up their heads. This phenomenon is an example of runaway sexual selection. Sometimes, a male with small antlers managed to breed in spite of himself and the species was thus almost—almost—saved from extinction. In some scientific circles, I have been told, this is called the "sneaky fucker phenomenon." Really.

In 1950, there were 153,000 public schools in the United States with enrollments of 25 million students, according to the federal *Digest of Education Statistics*. Today, there are 84,000 schools with a total enrollment of 41 million. While enrollments have nearly doubled, the number of schools housing all those kids has been cut nearly in half. Schools are much bigger than they once were. *Much* bigger. This has been done in the name of efficiency. The trend toward bigger schools accelerated greatly during the 1960s with release of a major study, *The American High School Today* headed by former Harvard University president James Conant. The study promoted the virtues of the large, comprehensive high school. It all sounded great: more elective choices, more and better equipment, fewer administrators, bigger antlers. And so our schools have consolidated, and so they have gotten bigger and bigger. But are they really more efficient? Are the big schools educating kids better for less money? Do electives, equipment, and systemization of administrative tasks produce better, more knowledgeable kids? Clearly, the public continues to believe they do. Our Lab School enrollments for the coming year were still only okay. The masses were not yet busting down the door to get in.

With scale has come standardization. "Objective" standardized tests have become the norm. Multiple-choice questions and factoid-based "essays" that are no more than a recital of concepts presented in class are the "industry" standard. At the same time, teachers have become ever more specialized working with an ever smaller aspect of a child's education. Thus kids spend their days in large anonymous institutions getting shuttled from one class to the next. No single adult in the institution really has a handle on who the child is, her strengths and weaknesses. And while the institution does a good job of measuring a student's ability to memorize and recite facts, it really has little sense of the student's ability to think imaginatively, work effectively with a group of classmates, solve a complex problem, conduct research, give an oral presentation, speak extemporaneously, or write a quality essay.

In August some of the Lab School teachers and Bethlehem administrators met with State Education Department officials to discuss in a preliminary way the prospects of a variance for the Lab School such that Lab School students might be granted a regents diploma. It was an interesting meeting. At the time, schools around the state were seeking and being granted waivers of regulations in the spirit of innovation and reform. Our petition was on a somewhat grander scale than most as we sought relief from all regents exams. Therefore, this preliminary meeting.

The state people were divided on our request. The representative from the Testing Bureau doubted the validity of our measures of student achievement. But others applauded our efforts to push kids to think hard and work together. The Testing Bureau insisted that a regents diploma, which we sought a variance for, is the result of passing prescribed tests for prescribed courses. I held that a regents diploma is whatever the Board of Regents deems their best standard and that they set up this variance process precisely to break away from the convention of prescribed tests and courses. There was a good deal of mutual harumphing throughout the meeting and we departed questioning whether, even if our variance were approved, we would really want it if it would draw us into a closer relationship with the Education Department and all the bureaucratic hassles that would imply.

Ironically, the very day we held this meeting I received the results for my fourteen students who had taken the advanced placement exam in U.S. History. The results were poor. I was very disappointed. Eager to challenge my better students, I'd encouraged too many to sit for the exam, and had discovered in the course of the year that the advanced placement syllabus, laden with content, was directly at odds with the Lab School curriculum, which focused on fewer topics in greater depth. For the students, it was a low-risk challenge as reporting advanced placement scores to colleges is optional. But from a political standpoint, the results were certain to confirm the opinions of many skeptics and could be a real blow to the program. I was nervous about how this one would play out in the fall.

The kids returned to school on Thursday, September 8. Thank god for the kids, as some of the grown-ups were driving us nuts. The return of the students to Lab School was like a big reunion, much back slapping, hand shaking, and high fiving. We held our orientation conference at a nearby Catholic summer camp and quickly got back into the academic year. It was great to be working with the same kids. I already knew so many of their strengths and weaknesses. I knew when I was getting a phony excuse and when a student was struggling. One afternoon early in the year Michele and I were talking after the students had left for the day.

"All these kids need," said Michele, "is one caring and reasonably competent adult. That's all they need, and they'll learn." For the money we spend in public education addressing special needs, we have very little to show—because our efforts are misguided. We use our money to buy more experts to shrink our kids' heads, which generates lots of diagnoses and reports and divides the students' time among still more adults who spend ever less time per student. If, instead, we used the money to buy more regular classroom teachers, scale back school size, and purchase more conference time for teachers to reflect on their work, we would be miles ahead.

Community meeting got off to a slow start in September. The previous year's hot issues—grades, late policy, Student Judicial Council, the schedule, drugs on field trips—had lain dormant all summer, and I expected that they would quickly surface, but we were now consumed by the start up of new routines and new schoolwork. I wouldn't have minded except the new students' first experience with Lab School governance was rather flat. I took to giving homilies about how democracy isn't always bone-chilling excitement, but we needed a hot issue. It arrived in late September.

On reflection of the previous year's experience, the teachers decided to propose that students who were behind in two or more subjects would be excluded from weekly program, attending instead a study hall. We presented the idea at community meeting, indicating that we (teachers) would make the decision on this one but wanted student advice. Which we got. A vocal minority was dead set against it. Trevor, a new sophomore, argued that if weekly program is educational and related to the curriculum, then students ought not to be excluded from it. We replied that while weekly program is both of those, it is not as essential as the material in the core courses. After several opening salvos, students spoke up who agreed with the policy, arguing that if you did not want to miss weekly program, all you had to do was, well, your homework.

We started the new policy. Unfortunately and ironically, the program that week was a guest speaker on self-esteem and the twenty-odd kids who missed were the ones who most needed it. But the next week sixteen students missed and the next week nine students and the next week six. Trevor continued to raise the issue weekly in community meeting but to no avail. The policy was a proven success.

Meanwhile, the high school was feeling shock waves from a new get-tough discipline policy. A whole raft of new rules and tougher enforcement floated in with September, and the kids were up in arms. By October, discipline referrals reached a high of seven hundred (Imagine being one of two assistant principals facing that kind of caseload!) The faculty room was buzzing with how horrible student behavior was and this was the absolute worst we'd ever seen, and so on.

A comparison is unavoidable. In the year that Lab School got underway, discipline problems nearly disappeared. Why? Could it be that students and teachers discussed issues, and that students had a real voice? Could it be that working as a smaller community, we found we must get along? Indeed. The conventional get-tough approach is doomed from the start. People do not respond well to rules imposed suddenly without prior discussion—especially when they are so draconian. Unfortunately, the conventional high school is unwilling to devote time—real time, scheduled regularly into the school day—for students and teachers to discuss the issues. We can't afford the time, the argument goes. We need it for math and English, and Spanish, and social studies, and so on. The reasoning is penny wise and pound foolish, however, because the time gained by not scheduling discussion of issues is lost to classes distracted by discipline problems.

Academically, the Lab school was much more stable than during our first year. This was the second year through our grades 10-11 program and even though the course work was different, policies and routines were established. Our new colleague, Bill Wojcik, was a godsend. He bristled with good ideas, was a strong, gentle presence in the classroom, and was amazingly comfortable with the ambiguity that permeates life in Lab School. It was on his initiative that we began to really integrate the literature and history portions of the humanities. I was foolishly content to have us teach in isolation from one another maintaining only a parallel time line as we marched chronologically through Western and Middle Eastern history. Thankfully, Bill wanted more.

It began simply. Bill and I started eating lunch together every Friday and shared what we were doing in class. As a result, we began cross-referencing each other in class—"As your know from your reading of *Gilgamesh* in Mr. Wojcik's class . . ." or "As in the Neolithic revolution that you've been studying with Mr. Nehring." Even those simple comments got our students' attention. We were encouraged and pushed a little further. A unit on the rise of Islam was coming up, and as we shared readings and topics under consideration, an idea for a joint literature-history project took shape. The kids would work in groups to develop a travel guide for Americans visiting the Moslem world. They would also present their guide orally. The nice thing about this project was that, even as it integrated the curriculum, it allowed Bill and me to maintain our individual autonomy in our classrooms. I realized, then, that fear of losing my autonomy was at the heart of my reluctance to develop a more interdisciplinary program. After all, I liked being the sole proprietor of my classroom. Having to coordinate my actions with someone else might mean not only more work, but a loss of liberty and spontaneity. The discovery that we could integrate our courses and still be relatively independent was marvelous. The further Bill and I went with our modest experiment, the more kids responded. A synergy appeared where previously it hadn't existed.

Change was afoot in other courses as well. Summer had granted Sue the opportunity she longed for throughout the first year to completely revamp the math curriculum and regroup students according to their level of achievement. Additionally, she and Jane had spent a week at Brown University in a math-science seminar sponsored by the Coalition of Essential Schools. As the weeks passed, it became clear that Sue's ideas and efforts were paying off. Students who had been frustrated by too-difficult math as well as those who had been bored by too-easy math seemed to be adjusting to newly challenging programs. Despite the new tracking policy, every student still got a full three-year dose of math in Lab School and had to demonstrate proficiency in a number of target areas that Sue defined as the essential math curriculum.

We also now had our first class of seniors, and though we had laid out a curriculum over the summer, our senior courses felt as new and uncharted as the grades 10–11 program had felt the year before. The plan was to offer intensive miniseminars, seven to eight weeks each, on various topics through the end of the first semester. The second semester would be devoted to the senior internship and development of the senior thesis.

I began in September with a course we called "college prep." It offered guidance in the development of college applications and the location of potential internship sites. One area these students really needed to work on was presentations. They had no concept of what it meant to produce a clean document, be it a business letter, resumé, application form, or college essay. If there were *just a few* grammatical errors, strike outs, typos, that was good enough. And that everything should be typed was news to them. As we made initial inquiries for internships, their inexperience with the adult world was made embarrassingly apparent. Students who would be regarded generally as competent with school tasks did not know how to use a phone book. And when they got on the phone, they were embarrassingly weak at initiating a conversation, making an inquiry, and closing the conversation. We held practice phone conversation in class full of giggles and false starts.

In some ways, our seniors were so mature and capable and in others so very naive; so full of bravado masking an essential lack of experience with the world.

Meanwhile, Jane and Sue were having a grand time with the seniors jointly developing a physics-math unit involving the design, construction, and blast off of rockets. In the back of our heads though, the big question was college admission. We had spent much time over the summer finalizing our transcript. We corresponded closely with several college admissions representatives and had consulted with the high school guidance department as well. The transcript went through four or five drafts between the spring and fall of 1994, including one major revision. What everyone kept telling us was to find a balance between the readability of a conventional transcript and the richness of a portfolio/narrative transcript—a balance that avoided the shallowness of the former and the ponderous density of the latter. No one could tell us precisely where that balance lay, probably because it was different for every college. But by October, our final draft was in hand. Now it was up to our students to people our transcripts with academic lives worthy of college admission.

On the faculty front, there was still a major storm system. Much complaint from the core of antagonists over our staffing and now a beef over the variance request. It seems the central office had listed the Lab School design team as party to the group requesting the variance, when in fact the design team had not been involved . What was an oversight for central administration became a major brouhaha among the oppositional forces, who blew the event way out of proportion. The upshot was that the high school faculty as a whole would have to review the variance request before the Lab School could submit it. This was a major change midstream, and one that required a completely new tactic including a major informational campaign that would take months. With everything else vying for our attention, the variance request just wasn't important enough and so we decided to not pursue it. One of the reasons given by our antagonists against the variance was that the Lab School wasn't good enough. I am unaware of any program evaluation conducted by any faculty member, but somehow these folks felt they knew. The one set of hard numbers, of course, was the advanced placement results. And judging from this one test administered to less than one-third of the population, taking nothing else into account, one might draw this conclusion.

I was beginning to feel bitter toward certain individuals who, from my perspective, seemed to slam us in the stomach every time we started to get on our feet. This was no frame of mind from which one ought to lead the Lab School. My anger was taking a personal toll. In the course of our first year, I had managed to do some damage to myself and was being treated for a suspected ulcer and chronic skin rash (stress induced, suggested my doctor). There were occasional chest pains, too. I approached Jane about taking on the role of Lab School coordinator and she very graciously agreed. Did she understand what she was getting herself into, I asked. She assured me that she understood the pressure involved. We discussed the change with the full team and all agreed Jane would be fine in the position. I felt much better. Jane was up to the task. Her energy was up. She was positive, and as a former union leader she was accustomed to taking multiple blows without flinching. I could focus more on my teaching and long-range planning for the Lab School

Another godsend to the Lab School came in the form of our new teacher intern from Union College, Cynthia Butcher. Like our other new colleague, Bill, Cynthia's temperament was well suited to the Lab School. Working with Cynthia was a good exercise for us all as her novice questions regularly called us from our routinized mode of operation and forced us to justify our actions. Cynthia worked with my U.S. history class in the high school and also rotated among Lab School classes leading lessons and longer units. While Cynthia's presence did not substantially lighten the load—working with an intern teacher never does—she enriched our school and allowed us some added flexibility.

At the end of October, responsibility for teaching the "college prep" seminar for seniors passed from me to Jane and Sue. I was now scheduled to lead an intensive humanities seminar with the seniors for about twelve weeks. During the summer, I had settled on a course design different from anything I had ever tried. I called the course Contemporary Literature and Culture, and I left the selection of readings up to the class. Each student was to pick a book that had made a major impression on him or her. Then they were to each select an excerpt of about twenty pages, write a five-hundred-word synopsis of the entire work and find a short (one- to two-page) published biography of the author. The packages thus produced were to form the basis of the course. As a class we would read and discuss approximately one work per week. Weekly essay assignments would help cap the discussion and, additionally, each student was required to read in its entirety one of the selections and write a critical review.

The seminar worked splendidly. Because students had selected the works, their interest was high. Our discussions were thoughtful and impassioned as we discussed major life questions embedded in the readings: What is the nature of humanity, the meaning of death, good and evil, the nature of society, and more. Connections among the diverse works emerged spontaneously. We read Alex Haley's *Roots*, Pat Conroy's *Lords of Discipline*, Carlos Castaneda's *Journey to Ixtlan*, Milan Kundera's *Unbearable Lightness of Being*, and easier works: Robert Fulghum's *Everything I Need to Know I Learned in Kindergarten*, and *Chicken Soup for the Soul*. On the whole, our discussions were the best I have ever had with high school students. I found the seminar challenging to my own thinking and I know it was challenging for many of the students.

One of the final activities conducted with the seminar was a series of two full-day field trips to the research library at the state university in Albany, where the assignment was to develop a short research paper on any subject of the student's choice. My purpose was to acquaint the class with the kinds of library resources that they would have at college—where most of them would be in ten months. The exercise proved very beneficial. They learned to use the electronic card catalog, the CD ROM databases, and the periodical room. This was no small feat, as finding a book in a collection that consumes three full stories of stacks is a whole different experience from finding a book in the school or town library. I knew now that come September, no matter which colleges these students attended, they would stride confidently into the library and know how to use it.

Their behavior on these outings to the university was truly charming. They were at times like ducklings following closely behind mama duck (me), somewhat intimidated by the university environment. At other times they were all bluster and overconfidence, trying to appear like anything but the high school students they were. I felt like a parent to a family of teenagers who needed me but also didn't want to have anything to do with me. On the bus ride home the second day, they asked if they could call me Jim. I said no.

As summer turned to fall and fall to the winter of our second year, two insights found their way into my thoughts. One: the force of conventional schooling exerts its hold not only through institutional rules, but more importantly routine. In the Lab School, I had been freed of numerous rules, yet in the development of curriculum I had difficulty breaking out of habits well entrenched by so many years of forced allegiance to the rules. In designing the humanities curriculum for the tenth and eleventh graders the first year, I had traded in one content-heavy syllabus (the regents) and without any coercion had plunked another one (advanced placement history) right down in its place, overlooking our vision of a curriculum with less content and greater depth. Interestingly, it took a new teacher—one whose habits were only two years deep—to tease me away from a traditional reconceptualization of the curriculum and begin to integrate subjects.

The other insight is related. I began to understand the development of the Lab School from an evolutionary standpoint. I had naively anticipated during the design phase that, once in place, the Lab School would immediately be the radically reconceptualized approach to learning that we dreamed of. I was learning that we are embarked on a process that will take years. What we call "traditional" public school has been about a hundred years in the making, and any reconceptualization, no matter how zealously promoted, would take years to be realized. The Lab School would be, and remain, a dynamic and volatile enterprise for years. It was not just an initial phase; it was our school's mission.

# 11

As early as 1988, the Coalition of Essential Schools was discouraging the creation of the school-within-a-school as an education reform strategy. Bitter experience at various sites around the country had led to a belief that the school-within-a-school by its nature creates division, jealousy, fear, and general discord, thus jeopardizing the possibility of larger-scale reform. At other times and from other sources, I have heard a similar refrain—that the school-within-a-school is not the vehicle of choice for systemwide change. But I have come to disagree.

Consider the alternatives. Some schools attempt schoolwide change right from the start involving believers and skeptics alike. By the time these changes are instituted, they are often heavily watered down as a result of much compromising in order to appease the skeptics. In my own school, an attempt to create near heterogeneous grouping throughout the building met with such stiff opposition that three years after the move began we were virtually back to where we started. While the claim was being made that we had done away with tracking, it wasn't really so. The change, because it attempted to encompass everyone, became a mile wide and only an inch deep.

A second alternative might be to create an "alternative" school, that is, a school program completely autonomous of the other district schools, housed even in a separate building. Many alternative schools were established in the 1970s and seem to have evolved in several different ways, none of which is very satisfactory. Some were closed because they cost too much, or lost student sign ups; others still thrive today but have no impact on the larger system since, because they are separate, they have become invisible, and, in fact, lessen the chances of reform in the larger system by siphoning off all the reform-minded teachers, students, and parents, leaving the traditionalists contentedly alone. Still others continue to operate, but in name only since, in order to survive, they have been forced to compromise away their identity. They have become engulfed by the system. Finally, there are those alternative schools that survive by taking all the students that the larger system doesn't want—the so-called at-risk students. These alternative schools enjoy continued support because they are politically attractive. Teachers are thrilled to have the problem kids removed from their classes, and the district is happy to offer an option to parents whose kids aren't fitting in. Often, the curricula of these at-risk alternative schools are superior because the teachers are given virtual license to try anything. (A telling lesson about the virtues of school autonomy.)

Then there's the school within a school: troublesome, politically volatile, divisive. But, then again, if real change is going on, won't there inevitably be trouble? Remember, we are talking about an entrenched system, expert at deflecting change efforts. Indeed, I would be immediately skeptical of any reform heralded as significant that is not in some serious way embattled.

At the school level, what other options are there? None. At the district level and higher, other options offer themselves: magnet schools, schools of choice, or charter schools. Yet these alternatives are no less troublesome (maybe more so) than those at the local level. Take charter school initiatives. At a grander level, they, like a school within a school, rock the educational boat. That they do so is testimony to their significance. I had the opportunity to observe from a distance the creation of a charter school in Massachusetts. In 1994, the state of Massachusetts chose fourteen proposals from among some sixty applicants for charter schools across the state. The winners, charter in hand, were free to set up shop. Their funding would come from the districts where their students resided, with the school receiving the average per-pupil expenditure of the host district for each child they enrolled. The level of acrimony that quickly ensued was predictable and familiar to anyone versed in the politics of school reform. The superintendent of the district that was going to be most affected declared that taxes would have to be raised to offset the loss of dollars to the charter school. Critics argued the measure was a threat to public education as it siphoned away crucial resources from an already resource-poor institution. Others questioned the legality of using public money to fund "private" schools. Comfortably tenured teachers feared for their jobs.

The arguments were all bogus. Imagine a town where there had been just one supermarket for as long as anyone could remember. With no competition, prices had drifted up while service had become sloppy. Customers complained bitterly, but none had the wherewithal to change the situation. One day, a group of citizens in town decided to pool their resources, lease a vacant warehouse, and start their own grocery store. A nearly audible cheer went up around town. Then the owner of the established supermarket took out a full-page ad in the paper where he made the following appeal: "Due to the recent loss of patronage, we will be forced to raise our prices in order to continue to meet payroll and cover our physical plant costs. We regret any inconvenience this may cause our customers and we look forward to your continued patronage."

The old grocer would be laughed right off the page. Yet this was the case made by the school superintendent! That his points weren't immediately identified as ridiculous is only a sign of how comfortable we have become with the public school monopoly. I imagine the old commissars in the Soviet Union railed similarly as the Soviet system was dying, but despite all the ensuing turmoil, would anyone really want to go back?

Equally absurd is the argument that the charter school threatens public education. The charter school is public. It is chartered by the state and funded with tax dollars. It is not the kind of public school we are used to, but it is public.

People fearing for their jobs is a natural response but not in itself a reason to embrace or reject a major policy proposal, particularly when the proposal will create jobs in roughly equal number to those lost.

The arguments against the charter school were rooted more in fear—not fear for children, but fear for the comfortable equilibrium of an institution grown smug over its ability to fend off change. What I fear is that the political turmoil that surrounds charter initiatives will cause states to shortsightedly back off and abandon them (just as some would abandon the school within a school), when in fact turmoil is the very mark of their promise.

Meanwhile, college applications were becoming the preoccupation of our seniors—and their teachers. November through December is high season for submission of all materials. In our ongoing quest to find that elusive balance between readability and depth, we decided to narrow the portfolio portions of the transcript to just four representative works. Jane and Sue, in charge of the senior college prep course as of November were pushing and prodding the class through a process of selection, revision, and ultimately, the production of clean, impressive documents. Again, the manuscript standards of the class were an issue with some who naively judged messy work good enough. On reflection, though, our frustration in this area was a sure sign we were pushing the students past their accustomed standard. Ultimately, it was the portfolio concept that drove our insistence as well as their compliance. Yet another example of "the test" driving the curriculum, an inescapable fact of school life, which, if we construct good tests, works to our pedagogical advantage. College admission by portfolio was the good test driving our students to a higher standard and us to more frequent headaches. So be it.

Around this time, we heard several reports (from either students or colleges, I don't remember which) that the lack of a class rank notation on the Lab School transcript was a problem. How unfortunate that colleges have become accustomed to relying on the sorting devices of others in determining the suitability of candidates for their programs: the SAT, class rank, high school grades. How much more meaningful it would be for the college to inspect the work of the student, put her through her paces in an oral examination, and make their own judgment. Many colleges no longer even encourage interviews. There are reasons of course: too many applications, not enough time. I understand. But as the Lab School was pushing the limits of institutional change at the secondary level, we now found our efforts crashing against the institutional norms of higher education.

Also disturbing about the demand for class rank is the tacit assumption that in our system of education, some are bound to succeed while others are bound to fail. No matter how well or poorly one meets the objectives, one's success is measured against a relative standard. Thus our acceptance that some don't and won't learn in our schools is reinforced. The Lab School, by challenging all to succeed was a defiant voice (crying in the wilderness).

As a result of all the college work, we came into closer contact with the guidance department. We gained a greater appreciation of their work and their struggles. And they, I believe, came to a better understanding of what the Lab School was trying to do. At the beginning of December, we got a nice compliment. All juniors in the high school had been in for the "junior conference" and shortly thereafter, one of the guidance counselors commented to me that her Lab School juniors seemed particularly interested, involved, and inquisitive. The next day, Michele reported the same comment from another counselor who added that all the counselors had remarked it to each other.

And the next day, we got our first college admission. Yahoo! Though none of us should have been surprised, the experience was like that of an electrician who upon wiring a new circuit, tests it for the first time and happily observes the light bulb blink on at the far end. Several days later, news of two more admissions arrived. That made three: Western New England College, SUNY Plattsburgh, and Purdue. This was the best kind of news. From the standpoint of parents considering Lab School for their academically inclined children, college admission out of our program was the litmus test. Now we had something to show.

God sends us these successes to fortify us for the next blow, which was dealt only days later as we were gearing up for student enrollment season. Lab School promotion began with a mailing to all ninth-grade parents, including a letter inviting them to consider the program and a new glossy brochure (developed the previous summer). Next step was an in-school orientation for ninth graders organized through their English classes. Then came an evening meeting for parents followed by an optional two-period visit and tour of Lab School classes for students with serious interest. The previous year, the visits had been sloppily handled and there had been complaints from teachers. This year, therefore, we decided to cut the visit back from a full day to just two periods, have students sign up with parental consent forms in advance, and issue a list of the students to the faculty just as if we were running a field trip. To announce all this the guidance Department issued a memo to all teachers. That's when the trouble started. Supervisors complained to the principal, teachers complained to the head of guidance, and union stalwarts complained to their union reps.

The issue was equity. Was it equitable for the Lab School to offer during-school visits while other elective courses could not? But the Lab School was not a single-semester elective course. It was a three-year high school program, complete with its own transcript. It was new and experimental. It was crucial that families make an informed choice. But those who opposed our work would have nothing of it. To them, this was another example of the Lab School getting special treatment.

Our visits took place the following week without incident. Of the 150 students who indicated interest in the Lab School after our orientations program, 50 signed up to visit. The attrition of interest concerned us. We had hoped this year we would have to go to a lottery. But it looked as though this year, again, we would get just about enough students to stay afloat.

Why? Because we were new, we were still considered risky, particularly for academic kids. Would they get into college—a competitive college—from Lab School? Would the Lab School education fare them well in college? Word of our first admissions was only just getting out as freshmen were deciding to enroll, and the data was still very thin. On the other hand, students who were less academic considered Lab School too difficult. Word had gotten around that Lab School students had to work. Too risky for some, too tough for others, A revolution is not a tea party, Mao Zedong said. This was all going to take time. We would not have a lottery this year. Maybe not next year either. But we would, eventually.

About this time, education was getting some ink in headlines around the country over several standards projects that were coming to completion. The National Social Studies Standards Project and the federal government had each released a document at about the same time. Simultaneously, a New York State Committee issued a social studies report. All the new reports were instantly surrounded by the usual media commentators charging racial bias, gender bias, political correctness, political incorrectness, historical revisionism, and the like. All of which caused me to reflect once again on the standards question.

Take, for example, history curricula. Any attempt to impose history standards across schools, let alone every school in the nation, is ludicrous. History is not science. It is an interpretive discipline. Conclusions are rooted as much in values as they are in facts. And historical research is guided as much by the documents one does not choose as the ones chosen. Perspective and subjectivity are woven into the fabric of any historian's interpretation of history. To suggest that there ought to be one standard for history taught in all schools from year to year suggests a fundamentally flawed understanding of the nature of history. Inconveniently for policy makers, historians do disagree.

But let's suppose that we accepted the idea of a history standard.

Why does the debate rage over the content of the school curriculum only? Why must historians in only our elementary and secondary schools fall in step and march together to the same historical drumbeat? Why not historians who teach in our colleges and universities? Why aren't there state and federal committees seeking to impose a one best college curriculum? Is it that we don't care what goes on in our colleges and universities? Surely not, campuses are alive with debate over what ought to be taught and how to teach it. But the debate is centered on the campus, among the teachers and the students (where it ought to be). If a state or federal panel attempted to impose a universal list of history standards on all college history departments, there would be a riot. The cacophony of academic freedom arguments would be deafening. Why then, do policymakers attempt to do it at the school level? Is it because schools are publicly funded and therefore subject to public control (including bureaucratically derived mandates)? Yes, they are certainly public and subject to public control, but so are state universities and, to a greater extent than is commonly acknowledged, so are private colleges. So that's not the reason either.

It is a matter of trust. There is a fundamental distrust of local control, an antidemocratic presumption that local school people and local citizens are not bright enough or well educated enough or generous enough to work it out on their own. We should be outraged. Does a central bureaucracy hold a greater claim to wise and tolerant decisions than common folk and their communities? Certainly both bureaucracies and localities have made unwise choices in the past: the flawed welfare system is largely the result of federal and state decisions. On the other hand, institutionalized racism (Jim Crow, police corruption) has been largely the inglorious legacy of local control. There have been abuses at all levels, but, abuses aside, to whom should the greater presumption defer for matters of policy? Answer: to the smallest relevant political subdivision, if we really trust the idea of the republic.

There are other reasons, though, that drive this compulsion for large and lock-step standards. One is the illusory assurance that it gives to the adults in charge. If we can but settle on what must be covered, write it down, and bind it tidily between two covers, then we may rest, knowing that democracy and the culture are safe. But if the curriculum resides only in the curriculum guide and the smug omniscience of the curriculum writers and not in the minds and hearts of young people, then our democracy and our culture are not safe. We must stop defining the curriculum as what is to be taught and begin defining it as what our students have learned. If we do this, the curriculum will at once become less sweeping in it scope and more urgent in its implementation. We would stop this endless, esoteric tinkering with our curriculum guides and instead pour our energy into seeing that our students master something—anything—meaningful. If our students mastered any of the standards guides already out there, we would be miles ahead.

While the reason to establish lock-step history standards are merely specious, the results of their implementation are dangerous. A curriculum for the masses necessarily implies a test for the masses. And a test for the masses requires that it be easy to administer and score, as well as "objective." Ease of administration and scoring means necessarily multiple-choice questions and if essays, only the most trivial and factoid based (Identify three previously memorized causes of the American Revolutionary War). We know the test drives the curriculum. Thus, dumb test means dumb curriculum. Secondly, the desire to create an objective test for a subjective discipline will either fail or it will create the dangerous belief among our students that all history is only a matter of fact. There is no ambiguity, no meaning to make. Is this really what we desire?

Teaching in Lab School was evolving into an emotional diet of weirdly juxtaposed highs and lows. Working with our students was almost always positive even in the midst of our frustrations with them, for they were growing and developing; and, if one watched long and intently, one could actually observe—like the barely perceptible but significant movement of the hour hand—their growth. Growth was more dramatically apparent when one thought back over the months (remember what Karen was like in September?) or years (remember her last September?). We could think in years.

In contrast to our interactions with our students came the occasional encounters with some of our less charitable colleagues. The icy looks in the hallways, the complaints and disparaging remarks about our program (drain on resources, low standards, no order, they all do drugs) that rarely came to us directly but regularly went around us and which we heard second or third hand.

Most frustrating of all was the negative counseling of students that went on, with some of our colleagues urging ninth graders and their parents not to sign up: a program for losers; it won't last anyway. Thankfully there were also those colleagues who supported us: the quiet voices of encouragement, even from those who did not particularly endorse our philosophy but respected our courage for trying something new, for sticking our necks out.

Finally, to round out all this emotional weirdness, came the interest of outsiders: thoughtful people in neighboring districts who longed to change their schools, too. Shenendehowa and Saratoga, our neighbors to the north; the Albany city schools; and others. Also, area colleges: SUNY Albany, Union College, Rensselaer Polytechnic Institute, Siena College. And the media: our town newspaper, the Albany *Times Union*, Albany's public radio station, the local ABC-TV affiliate. The interest from outsiders was positive and most encouraging. The day the Saratoga visitors were in, we invited a group of students to join them for a chat. We (teachers) sat rapt and just listened as our students answered the visitors' most direct questions.

"Has the Lab School helped you become more organized?"

Karen, a spirited sophomore answered, "Definitely. I used to be like totally unorganized. I never did homework—well, hardly ever— and just kind of hung out, watched TV, you know. Now I have to organize my time. I can go out maybe two nights a week. I'm definitely working harder and the thing is, I like it.

"Why do you like it?"

Jared, a junior who'd been with us two years answered, "We like Lab School because we're among friends. I know if I have a problem with an assignment I can call anybody. I mean it, anybody, and they'll help me. And these are people that in regular school I never would have gotten to know 'cause they weren't in my click."

"Do you still have friends in the regular school or do you feel cut off?"

"I feel I have friends. Sure." This was Sharon, a shy and interesting sophomore. "In fact I think because I'm in Lab School, I've learned more about friendship and my bond with my other friends are stronger."

"What about academics?" Are you learning?"

"I'm definitely learning." Aaron, uncharacteristically quiet until now. "I sat through earth science last year and literally slept for half of the course and I got an A. This year I'm working my buns off and I'm getting 4s, you know, like, Bs."

"And that doesn't bother you?"

"No. It really doesn't. I mean, I'm learning. I'm enjoying it. I know that sounds weird, but its really true."

The interrogation continued in the same vein a good forty-five minutes. Our visitors were incredulous. We were struck dumb. Surely, we were on to something here. If only our skeptical colleagues could hear and see this, we commented later. Then, no. Seeing this would not persuade them. Nothing would. Essentially, their opposition was rooted in feelings, not reasons. "How come the Lab School gets all the attention? My program, which I've labored over for years, is great and nobody's ever noticed me; or, the deepest and largely unspoken feeling, My god, am I going to have to rethink everything I do? I've spent years getting this job under control. I vowed to never again endure those sixty-hour first-year-teacher weeks. No thank you. One of the union officers had commented that the collegial antagonism over Lab School was essentially a sibling rivalry, peers vying for attention, recognition, gratitude. An apt analogy.

The first semester closed with the parade of examiners and student orals—our third time through the process. Our state assemblyman, John Faso, an attorney with a quick mind and scholarly bent, made a return appearance—he had attended our first round of exams the previous January—and commented with odd surprise betraying a genuine sincerity that the presentations were considerably improved this time around. Also attending, for the first time, was Harry Rosenfeld, editor-in-chief of Albany's daily newspaper, the *Times Union*. An older gentlemen, appropriately gruff in demeanor for a man whose career was forged in the news room, he strode into the examination room, leather brief case clutched at his side, held forth in his assigned role, and, with little comment, left at the end of the morning session. To our great delight, this editorial appeared several days later in the Sunday edition of his paper under the headline, "A Special Program At Bethlehem High."

Education is a major American frustration. Almost wherever we look, we find lower achievements by students and higher cost for taxpayers.

Articles in the media endlessly analyze the problem and debate solutions, which remain fragmentary at best but mostly elusive.

At Bethlehem Central High School, however, they've been doing something special about education for a couple of years. A four-hour visit there last week, to serve as an evaluator of student projects, leaves a participant optimistic about possibilities.

The program is called the Lab School. It is a school within the larger context of a normal suburban high school with an ample campus, a large parking lot, and a long-standing reputation as a quality community institution.

The Lab School selects it participants from the general student body. Unlike other programs, it is not limited to the brightest.

Its very inclusivity is the Lab School's defining essence that should speak loudly to the rest of the world. Elsewhere, programs for the best and better students have fallen victim to educational egalitarianism and occasional charges of racial exclusiveness. As a consequence, the people who would most benefit society by having their minds challenged to the utmost are deprived of the opportunity.

Although everyone gets the chance to apply for the limited program, which runs from the sophomore year, all must meet the same set of standards, which the program makes clear are high. If a student is not the swiftest deer in the herd, he or she will have to put in extra effort, including summer work, to keep up.

The program is kept small, with its own faculty. Impressive is the coherence among teachers and students, the participation for parents, and, of course, the behind-the-scenes support of administrators.

The relationships among these groups, but especially the self-supporting dynamics that emerge from students working shoulder to shoulder and meeting faculty on what appears to be more relaxed terms results in obvious accomplishments.

Part of the Lab School year involved students undertaking research papers along with five or so of their peers. Each writes on a subject and all team members are expected to be grounded in every one else's work, enough to be able to discuss it intelligently.

There comes the day when a panel of evaluators, including the faculty and outside guests, who have read and graded essays prepared by the students, is convened to hear oral presentations and to ask questions.

Students are expected to integrate visual aids and they are judged not only on the content but on their manner of presentation.

For a moment being a part of the Lab School was instructive not only in witnessing what can be done in the real world with available means. It was also informative in substance. One essay, for example, argued that the fall of the Roman Empire was attributable to the noblest sopping up lead-poisoned wine (becoming infertile as a consequence). Another reported on an advanced civilization, the Moche which existed in South America before the Incas. A third analyzed the mathematics of sound and music.

One Lab Schooler spent four months in Russia as an exchange student. Her reports, written and oral, were vivid, humane and knowing.

Asked what she intended to do in the future with her acquired Russian expertise, she answered she would like to be a journalist working as a correspondent in Russia.

We should only be so lucky.

# 12

Some schools aspire to be child centered. They strive to understand the child's interests, talents, and weaknesses beyond the narrower context of academic achievement in an effort to promote the growth and development of the whole child—a worthy aspiration, indeed, one that ought to drive the work of any school and, we regularly reminded ourselves, should drive our own work. In the spring of its second year, the Lab School began to surge beyond its child-centered focus, and due to the initiative of a committed core of Lab School parents, started to suggest the exciting possibilities of a school that is family centered.

Progressive educators dating back to John Dewey and Maria Montessori have emphasized the importance of educating the whole child. While this tenet finds some allegiance in American elementary schools where children are given relative space to explore, experiment, and be understood as persons, the compulsion to force feed traditional academic subjects gradually usurps the finite time of the school day until, by the time a young person reaches high school, almost no attention is given to his personhood as each course of prescribed curriculum is dished up eight periods per day, 180 days per year.

High school programs that attempt to reach the whole child are viewed as soft, academically second rate, coddling. Certainly, the Lab School has suffered from that perception as it is the view of many outspoken traditionalists on the high school faculty, some of the key opinion leaders, the professors. This view is unfortunate because it hobbles fledgling programs trying to gain acceptance. Sometimes, it destroys them. It is unfortunate, also, because it is wrong. No one gains inspiration in a humanless vacuum. Everyone who succeeds does so in large part because someone has reached out to that person, taken an interest in her, believed in her, liked her. Listen to valedictory speeches, commencement addresses, retirement speeches, and award acceptance speeches and you will hear the emotion-choked tributes: so-and-so reached out to me, so-and-so believed in me, so-and-so has been my mentor. Listen carefully and you will hear also in the phrasing, and the pauses, an implication that these crucial human contacts, these expressions of faith, occur in spite of circumstances, when everybody else was too busy, along the margins of a school life so filled with other study that reaching out to someone in a human, caring way was the exceptional event.

If we recognize that basic caring is the crucial ingredient in the success of our most successful citizens, why do we not promote it more in schools? Why do we not make an institutional commitment of time and resources to see that each student can feel, as apparently only some lucky ones currently do, the assurance that somebody cares about them, believes in them, has time for them?

But perhaps this is a responsibility that is better left to the family. Is the demand that schools become more personal and nurturing really just a desperate effort to compensate for the erosion of quality family life? It is a family responsibility, to be sure, and, while no one can deny that the contemporary American family is in serious trouble, schools ought to reach out to the whole child even under the best of family circumstances. A parent is a child's first mentor and friend, but to succeed at later stages of growth, particularly under circumstances where a parent's presence is not primary, a child needs others to step in to provide guidance and support.

Unfortunately, the modern guidance counselor (an apparent commitment by the institution to provide nurturing and support) is not in a position to do this on a regular basis. With case loads usually well over 250, heavy demands to manage student schedules, even the most committed counselor will find it impossible to counsel most or even half her students on a regular basis.

Indeed, a small school with a cohesive teaching team and the opportunity to work with students for more than just one year is the only institutional arrangement that naturally promotes nurturing relationships. Beyond the structural matter of size, though, even a small school must make a curricular commitment to the establishment and maintenance of community among teachers and students through advisory groups, community meetings, shared decision making, team-building retreats, and the like. They are essential and they do indeed take time from math and social studies and English class. But, in the long run, an investment in community will pay off with improved academic results as well.

When the Lab School parents spontaneously organized the Lab School Parent Support Group in December of our second year, we began to learn about the possibilities of pushing a child-centered school one step further. For example, parents wanted to become more involved with the twenty- and forty-week projects. We had encouraged each student group to seek out a parent coach, and the expression of interest from the parent group pushed us to formalize the relationship. Each group was required to have a coach and the coaches began conversing with the teachers about group progress. More parents were showing up at the exams and more students were feeling comfortable with their parents' presence—no small miracle given the strains of most parent-teen relationships. The second annual pasta dinner held in March was another opportunity, provided by the parents, for families to work productively together. Then, in April, the parent group organized a potluck dinner to welcome new families to the Lab School. Cynthia and her husband Paul, both professional contra dance callers organized a dance for the event. The level of comfort among parents, students, and teachers all working together in each other's presence was moving; education became powerfully motivating for all parties. When I consider the almost total nonrelationship that characterizes the student-parent-teacher triad in most high school settings, the contrast is almost upsetting. So much educational potential stands untapped in conventional schools. And so much mistrust and negativity needlessly preoccupies the energies of all parties.

Meanwhile, the spring semester was bringing us a new curricular challenge: senior internships. Here, too, the beneficial effects of parent involvement were being felt. As the semester began, our placements were nearly complete, many of them the result of intervention by a parent. Sean, interested in traditional Eastern health practices, was placed with an M.D. nearby who blended Indian and Western medicine in her practice. Jonathan, interested in diet and vegetarianism, found a placement at a whole foods restaurant in Albany. Claire was placed with a professor at RPI where she would help with water pollution research and take an introductory chemistry course. Paul would be working with a county judge. Sue found a placement at the student counseling center at SUNY Albany. Karen floundered for several weeks unable to nail down anything that really interested her. Finally, through her ties to a Buddhist organization in nearby Grafton, she became interested in a peace march that was to take place for ten weeks and cover one thousand miles starting in Plymouth, Massachusetts, circling Lake Ontario and ending at the United Nations headquarters in New York City, where marchers would rally in support of renewing the nuclear nonproliferation treaty. We were skeptical, but Karen insisted this was for her. Thankfully, her advisor Michele, took the project seriously and worked hard to obtain permission from the school district for what became our most extraordinary internship.

True to our predictions, and what Vic Leviatin—the founder of the Westchester Individualized Senior Experience (a successful high school internship program)—had suggested, most of our placements resulted from either direct or indirect personal connections. Jonathan had eaten at the whole foods restaurant and had introduced himself to the chef owner. A Lab School parent in the health field made initial contact with the medical doctor. Jane drew on her contacts at RPI to help place Claire, and so on. Vic was indeed right in asserting that grassroots networking was a much easier and more efficient approach to building an internship program than any kind of institutional approach. It also made the student practically responsible for the placement, giving him or her a greater stake down the road in seeing it through. Were the student to quit the internship or slack off, she would be disappointing her friends, family members, or teachers.

But all was not perfection along the internship road. We encountered some bumps. During the spring semester, a portion of the senior seminars was devoted to an ongoing discussion of the internship . One day in late February, Maria began class by complaining that for her internship at the recording studio so far, all she had done was answer the phone and file papers. And, she continued, she was growing weary of feigning cheerfulness on the phone when she, and everyone else at the studio, was generally in a foul mood. Deborah, interning for a large retail chain headquartered in Albany, lodged a similar complaint. "I've been doing nothing but putting price stickers on CDs for two weeks, working under some guy who I don't think even graduated from high school." Other seniors reported similar disappointment, raising in general two issues. First, I fear our students' expectations were in some instances unrealistic. Given the world of work as portrayed on TV, Deborah might have envisioned a corner office with a view, frequent trips to L.A. on the corporate Lear jet, client lunches at four-star restaurants, and a pocket cellular phone for making deals between meetings. Putting stickers on CDs was not part of the anticipated routine. And Maria and Deborah were not the only ones disappointed by their work routines. Nearly half complained to some degree of the same problem. As gently as we could, we alerted them to the facts of the working world—that most jobs, no matter how exciting, involve some degree of routine, and even occasional drudgery, that you just make the best of it and learn from it, and that demonstrating initiative with the tasks you are given will help you to get noticed and move up.

All of which raised a second, closely related and more legitimate issue. Were our students being exploited by their intern sponsors for their free labor? If, after all, the internship involved nothing more than putting stickers on CDs, then it was not the kind of experience we wanted for our seniors. The difficulty lay in figuring out how much of what we were hearing was adolescent griping and how much was evidence of exploitation. Maybe, after all, some of the intern sponsors were only starting our student out with menial jobs so they wouldn't wreck anything and, as they proved themselves, they might be given more responsibility. We explored this possibility, too, with the seniors, pointing out that a glum outlook toward work they were given would only ensure more menial jobs.

Another issue, knottier still, arose from Sean's internship with the medical doctor. It began with the suggestion by Sean that the practice was charging too much money for instruction in meditation/relaxation techniques. At first, I dismissed this as the shock of an innocent encountering for the first time the price scale of health care in America. But Sean insisted it wasn't right. Other instructors in the same technique, he claimed, regularly charged $35 for lessons, not $600. Two weeks later, Sean expressed a new concern of a nearly cultlike attitude among the medical staff where he was training. The Indian guru who they revered was treated, Sean claimed, with nearly worshipful deference. He was, they said, ageless and immortal. With this, I made a phone call to the practice but was unable to ferret out anything substantial, probably because I was being overly tactful—after all, the internship sponsors were helping us out, they were providing a service to us on a completely voluntary, pro bono basis. So I was reluctant to appear demanding or critical. At the same time I had a responsibility to look out for my students.

A week later Sean came to my classroom early one morning and announced abruptly that he quit his internship. I was at once angry at him for taking this unilateral action (I had considered it a real coup to have found a medical practice in the area for Sean that coupled Eastern traditions with Western practices) and concerned that his charges were more urgent than I had been ready to believe. I tried to express both aspects of my reaction to Sean, but I think the former came across louder and clearer. Sean's action seemed so cavalier, so ungrateful given the efforts by several people to find and maintain his placement. "Internships don't grow on trees," is, I think, the phrase

I used. But Sean assured me he had other options, among them, a kung fu master from whom he was already receiving instruction.

Then, about a week later, Maria came by my room with an identical early-morning announcement. In her case, it was the "hypocrisy of the business world" that she chose to no longer tolerate, the "phoniness." Again, her unilateral decision angered me as had Sean's. Again I was left wondering, was this the rash decision of a spoiled adolescent or the principled choice of someone who knows who she is and is willing to take the consequences?

I was worried that we would be unable to find new placements for Maria and Sean. I was concerned also that their precipitous act might move their classmates to do likewise and we would soon have an internship rout. But it worked out. Maria and Sean both met and spoke with their internship sponsors to explain their departures (I had urged them to do this and was proud of them for following through), and both managed to work themselves into new internship experiences—Maria with a local Montessori preschool and Sean with the kung fu master. The senior year was proving to be a learning experience for us all.

Another major event, not a happy one, during the winter months was the sudden departure of our math teacher, Sue. We had expected it to happen as she is a talented person who was working in a part-time replacement position. It was only a matter of time before a tenure-track math position would open up somewhere in the region. It happened in December. Sue applied for and got a great job in a nearby school district that was zooming ahead with heterogeneous grouping and portfolio assessment as the only Albany area member of the Coalition of Essential Schools. We were thrilled for Sue and a little envious, but her departure created a vacancy that would not be easy to fill. What sort of teacher would we be likely to find in December for a part-time, replacement position with a new politically embroiled program struggling to get on its feet?

We got lucky. Very lucky. Patty came to us via a successful student teaching experience just completed with our own high school math department. She was inexperienced but enthusiastic and energetic. Her substantial talents became apparent, and over the course of her first month or two our collective sigh of relief turned to a nod of real approval. The acid test was an evening meeting held in January, attended by about 150 parents and students. A competent teacher can handle a class full of students, but only a really good teacher can handle a room full of their parents! Patty spoke well and deftly handled their questions. The math program had weathered the transition and was again on its way.

I remain in a quandary over the subject of math. We had concluded, based on our first year's experience, that students ought not to be taught math in heterogeneous groups. The better students were bored, the weaker students became frustrated and those in the middle were distracted by the other two groups, who had stopped paying attention. So, during the summer between our first and second years, we had divided the kids into three groups, which seemed to be a natural division of their strengths. As a result, the second year started out much more smoothly. The students were more comfortable and so were their parents. We were, too. I wonder, though, if we were placing too high a value on comfort and retreating too quickly to old habits. While the results of our approach during the year warranted change, had we acted more out of desperation than imagination? Are there legitimate alternative possibilities for math instruction in a heterogeneous context. Are there completely different conceptualizations of math that we are missing?

At the same time, we had to act responsibly. We were not working with white mice; these were real people and somebody's children. In the event of problems, retreating to the traditional was not just a desperate move, it was also a responsible move. Which raises a related issue: How far may we push the envelope and still be able to operate in the real world of public education? It is an issue that goes well beyond the boundaries of mathematics instruction and becomes an issue because of two essential constraints. The first is the constraint of our responsibility to serve our clients well. We do not have complete freedom to employ whatever methodology we choose. While we enjoy relative autonomy compared with most mainstream schools, our priorities are, first, to serve our students well and, second, to innovate. While the two are not always antonyms (indeed, given the state of public education they may more often be synonymous), it is essential that we keep the priorities right. The second constraint comes from the first. The institutional settings from which our students come (elementary school, middle school) and to which they are headed (college mostly) dictate much of what we may do and may not do. In math, as an example, students come to us with a wide range of abilities—the result as much of native intelligence as much as the number of tracks into which they have been placed over the years. By the time they reach tenth grade, our students have been tracked into five math levels. As much as we may want to alter the traditional curriculum, we are limited by the fact of their widely varying levels of experience. (Of course, there may be a latent advantage to their varied experience we simply have not yet figured out.) In other subjects, too, students come to us with widely varying proficiency. Just as the lower grades deal us a hand over which we have no control, so too, the expectations of higher education pressure us to provide certain experiences for our students, again constraining our freedom to innovate. Colleges want SATs, class rank. They want recognizable course names and scores. Thus we are constantly living the questions: How far may we go? When do we back off? Like an Indy race car driver we want to take the turns at the fastest possible speed without hitting the wall. Judging what is one mile per hour less than the speed at which the tires lose their grip of the road surface is the high-stakes/high-stress enterprise that defines our work.

As winter turned to spring, and district attention turned to the next year's budget, the parent support that had become so significant to the educational program now became a force for increased staffing and student enrollment. The budget season began with the gloomy news from newly elected Governor George Pataki that state aid to schools would be frozen at the current year's level. Figuring for inflation, that actually meant a decrease in state aid to localities. The prospect was gloomier still for Bethlehem because enrollments districtwide stood at the beginning of a projected ten-year upward trend resulting in 40 percent overall growth.

The Board of Education responded predictably by asking principals and department supervisors to find 3 percent worth of cuts in the programs. This resulted in much general discord, but the cuts were made and presented to the board, which then spent the remainder of the budget season hearing arguments to restore funding. The Lab School was slated for a staffing reduction of 0.4 FTE—which means four-tenths of one teacher, or two of us each taking on an additional high school class. On the one hand, we fully expected this anyway. The board had granted us a .4 increase the previous July with the clear understanding that it was a one-year temporary measure to help us get our first class of seniors into college. On the other hand, the withdrawal of staffing was perceived by the community (which was not well-versed in the history of the staffing increase) as a withdrawal of support for the program. No doubt this was a negative factor in the decision of ninth-grade families considering Lab School enrollment for their children. It also presented multiple dilemmas for us. We certainly wanted to protect our program, but we also had to be honest with parents who wanted an explanation for the staffing cut. In being honest, however, we ran the risk of appearing weak, of caving in to the board decision without a fight. Also, we had to consider the faculty response. Given the level of faculty disapproval that accompanied the staffing increase the previous year, it would be politically correct to take our lumps and adopt an appropriately solemn attitude.

Given all of the above, and given the undesirable nature of all the scenarios it presented, we decided to create a different alternative. It went this way: Lab School staffing was tied to high school staffing by way of a formula that would give us an "average" student load. Therefore, if high school staffing increased, ours would, too. While it would create tremendous strain with the faculty to lobby for Lab School staffing when other departments were staying flat or experiencing cuts (especially since a full-court press might get us what we needed), it would do us no harm to lobby for increased staffing of the high school in general. In fact, if we and our parents were out front publicly promoting schoolwide, even districtwide staffing increases, it might help ameliorate relations with some of the faculty. The board's obvious affection for the Lab School could thus, in the eyes of teachers, be turned from a source of jealousy to a benefit for all.

Our parents had already begun a vigorous campaign to help the Lab School through letters to the board and local paper, a presence at meetings, and public speeches at meetings. Their Lab School centered efforts were already creating a mild faculty backlash that would inevitably grow to a tidal wave unless we did something fast. As quickly as we could, we got the word out to parents. Gradually, they came to understand the wisdom of this alternative strategy and with remarkable restraint turned their lobbying efforts toward the interests of the whole school.

Meanwhile, there was rumbling from the administrative team that the Lab School teachers had better stop organizing the parents. We were not, we insisted, organizing. In fact, we pointed out, we were attempting to educate them so as to avoid any potentially damaging actions. The charge was really rather flattering though. The idea of parents lobbying with such vigor and in such numbers for an academic program was unusual. Surely, logic dictated, it must be a carefully orchestrated tactic led by the teacher. However, we were not the initiators.

Having to persuade parents to not lobby on behalf of our program is ironic when one considers the effect that a staffing reduction would have on our students and on our day-to-day work lives as teachers. I want to call it crazy, as many do, but in fact it is not. It is complex. And the only way for our program to succeed would be to acknowledge the complexity, as we always had, and to craft equally complex strategies. While the temptation is sometimes great to start throwing hand grenades, they will inevitably make more enemies who sooner or later will demand a comeuppance. One is better served by a Gandhi-like approach, for he rightly understood that the only permanent solution to conflict is moral persuasion. It is important, he said, to maintain good relations with your adversaries for the sake of that future day when you will dwell together peacefully.

Meanwhile, the sophomores and juniors were already thinking about the forty-week presentations. At twenty weeks, several examiners had expressed concern or disappointment at the frequency of typos, grammatical errors, and spelling errors in the papers. Considering the name of the project ("twenty-week report"), they felt the paper really ought to be free of such cosmetic problems. (The truth is, of course, that the students had not spent twenty weeks on their papers—but that is not an excuse.) The errors suggested a careless attitude in general, implying maybe sloppy research and other more serious procedural problems. Our students were aware of this criticism. Some of it had been shared in a panel discussion with the examiners immediately following the exams. Other comments made to us had been conveyed to the students at community meeting. It was during a community meeting where such a discussion was going on, that one student boldly offered that maybe they should write two drafts prior to submission of the final copy instead of just one, as had been required. The idea seemed to quickly resonate with others and before the end of the meeting, we had agreed by consensus that for the June papers two drafts and a final copy would be required.

As the idea was taking shape during the course of the community meeting, I felt growing satisfaction. The usual scenario under these circumstances would be for the teacher to insist over great student protest that they must pen an additional draft. There would be no enthusiasm for the idea and only partial compliance yielding ultimately only questionable results. These students were suggesting the ideas to us, asking, would it be all right if . . . It was a simple statement suggesting a profound and favorable shift in the learning process. Indeed, our students were claiming responsibility for their education.

Adjunct to the discussion about three copies of the research report was a two-part request by the students that they form their groups sooner (the norm had been ten weeks before the exams)—right away, so that they could get to work on their projects—and that they be allowed to form their own groups. In the past, the teachers had formed the groups with input from students about who they wanted to work with. The request to start sooner was, like the request for three drafts, a delight to our ears, but we were initially hesitant about the other idea because our ability to match students of complementary strengths and to use the groups to address various personality issues had been quite helpful. We also feared some students would be left out after groups were formed.

But the kids pressed us, and given their very responsible request for three drafts, we decided to grant their wish. Thus began a lengthy process which, while it resulted finally in student-selected groups, taught our students some unanticipated lessons in the complexity of group dynamics. We told the kids their work would not be done until everyone was in a group. Initially, we devoted a double-period block to the process. The students understood that simply selecting a friend would not be appropriate so we came up with a gimmick to help shuffle the deck a little. Each student wrote some prescribed information about his/her strengths, weaknesses, interests, and personality on the face of an index card. The cards were taped to the wall around the room—no names attached—and everybody browsed the gallery noting numbers (each card was assigned a number) of persons they thought would make good group partners. We then revealed the names and let the groups form. By the end of the period we did not have ten complete groups. We had chaos. We agreed to devote the next community meeting to continuing the process. Despite everyone's best efforts, the job was not done even after that. It wasn't until we had spent another double block that the groups were finally formed. The teachers by then were quite anxious about the amount of school time spent on the process and the students were ready to accept that forming groups is not a simple matter, and maybe the teachers ought to do it.

It was around this time, early March, that the Lab School/district staffing issue began to heat up. With the climate of activism swirling around the Lab School teachers and parents it would have been impossible for it to not also affect the students. And so, at community meeting, the kids began to ask, How many kids are signed up for next year? Who will be teaching in Lab School next year? How many high school classes will Lab School teachers teach? How does enrollment influence staffing? Does the high school faculty support the program? What's this about a high school faculty vote? What can we do to support the Lab School? All great questions. All of which caused the teachers to ask, What is our appropriate role in answering them? On the one hand, it made perfect sense for the students to become politically involved in the fate of their school. They had at least as great a stake as anyone else. Involving them was consistent with our commitment to student involvement in school governance. And, as we had learned from similar experience in the last two years, a crisis could provide a unique opportunity for learning, a teachable moment. On the other hand, there were reasons to not involve the students. They were after all our students, not our political operatives. To employ them in a partisan conflict smacked of exploitation, a violation of the respect teachers must maintain for the freedom of their students' minds. Also, in our very traditional school, the idea of involving students in staffing and budget decisions was completely alien. To introduce the concept at a moment when the stakes were so high could be political suicide.

As matters evolved, we took a middle path. When students asked questions, we provided answers. There ought at least to be an open sharing of information about how the system works. But if they asked for advice about what they should do, we refrained from offering it.

We helped them to consider the possible consequences of various actions, but we stopped short of recommending what to do.

I often wanted to tell the students to fight like hell, attend and speak up at every board meeting, confront the teachers who had told them not to sign up for Lab School, and write to all the newspapers. In fact, we resisted, but they wound up doing most of the above anyhow. They were a presence along with their parents, sometimes vocal, at board meetings throughout the budget season. Tracy Detweiler, a junior, wrote a beautiful letter to *The Spotlight*. Several confronted teachers who had advised them not to join. And several students who were politically more astute began counseling their peers, even as we could not, to attend board meetings in numbers, recruit more ninth graders, be vocal, and be active. We, the teachers, all silently cheered their eloquent appeals.

In the end, the staffing debate resulted in the Board of Education adding 2.6 new teachers to the high school, and when we ran the formula to determine Lab School staffing, the high school increase brought us a one-tenth increase—which meant that Bill Wojcik moved from a .4 to .5. Though one-tenth sounds insignificant, to a program consisting of 3.2 teachers, struggling to devise a schedule that gives every student what they need and still stay within contractual guidelines, one-tenth is very significant. It was the half a loaf that kept us from starving. As spring got underway our newly formed family-centered school was finding some reasons for optimism. We were not yet out of the woods, but we were beginning to imagine the possibility of a clearing ahead.

The year came, as it always does, to a swift conclusion. May and June were consumed with preparation for exams and the closing conference, which we were to hold at Silver Bay YMCA Camp on Lake

George just as we had the previous year. We decided that as a major portion of the conference we would involve the students in a year-end program evaluation. Dividing them into focus groups, we set aside a two-hour session at Silver Bay for each group to explore a range of issues from courses to teachers to scheduling, community meeting, and so forth. As a school we had agreed on the topics weeks earlier. The focus groups were run by seniors, and teachers sat in to watch and intervene as needed. When a teacher's course came under review, the teacher left the room. The focus groups then met all together to report out in sessions that we held at the high school the following week—the last week of school. The candor and maturity that students demonstrated in the focus groups and the large group sessions was impressive. They seemed comfortable offering criticism with the teachers present (such was the level of trust) and praise without embarrassment. It was a satisfying conclusion to our second year.

# 13

*A Talk to the Lab School delivered at the 1995 End-of-the-year Banquet*

There is a program on National Public Radio called *Car Talk* where these two guys with thick Boston accents yuck it up as they abuse callers with car problems. At the end of the show they run the credits and after about the third name you realize all the names are made up. My favorite is their director of strategic and long-range planning: Kay Sera.

Three summers ago, Michele Atallah, Jane Feldmann, and I were sitting around a table facing the overwhelming task of launching a new school. We decided we should each have a title. Partly out of modesty but mostly out of fear of taking the blame, none of us wanted to be president. So we all became vice presidents, and declared Les Loomis our president—that way we could always say, "It's not our fault." Jane became vice president for public relations because she's good with big groups of people; Michele became vice president for accounting because she's great with money; and I became vice president for strategic long-range planning because I usually have my head in the clouds.

Therefore, since it's my job, anyway, I want to say a few words tonight about the long term, about where we've been as a school and where we are going.

The story is told of the man who had his head in a hot oven and his feet on a block of ice. He was asked, how did he feel? He replied, on average, I feel pretty good.

I've come to the realization that like the man, the Lab School finds itself in two very different places at the same time, and that while both places are interesting, they really don't balance each other out.

Like the crew of a ship on an uncharted sea, we've been sailing along now for two years, figuring things out as we go, relying on each other's wits, ingenuity, and patience to solve problems, and amazingly, we find ourselves today afloat, sails trimmed, good breeze, moderate seas. It is because of this relative calm that I've had the opportunity in recent weeks to reflect on where we are, who we are, what we are.

This program began seven years ago with a group of teachers who like many of you were not comfortable with things as they were. Our discontent was difficult to articulate, though we tried. We were like a young couple who knows they want a child yet they have little idea what that child ought to grow up to become. And that was as it should be—a school, like a child, ought to have a life of its own. It ought to be guided more by shared values and careful, continuous rethinking, rather than codes and policies developed by remote authorities at some earlier date.

So, one day this child appeared. All of a sudden, there was the Lab School. I remember our first day two years ago. We took a picture of everyone up in room 55-57. Everybody smiled at the camera and said "anxiety." It was like a birth, full of excitement and nerves and so much naïveté. If we'd only known then what we know now—what parent has never said that!

So what do we know now? We certainly know a lot about school politics—politics that constantly swirl around us and at times in the last two years have threatened to overturn us. But we have bailed mightily, mended sails, clung to the rigging, clung to each other, guided I guess more by faith than by any reason I can fathom, and very few of us have run for the lifeboats.

But this is not a speech about school politics. I don't know about you but I am weary from lobbying, petitioning, persuading, assuaging, calculating full-time equivalents, running formulas, and avoiding land mines.

My remarks today are about philosophy, about shared beliefs, about the very heart of our little school. How often do we get the chance to talk about that? How often do we think about it? Not often enough.

Sixty years ago, John Dewey, the parent of progressive education wrote, "The more a teacher is aware of the past experiences of students, of their hopes, desires, chief interests, the better will he understand the forces at work that need to be directed and utilized for the formation of reflective habits" (*How We Think*, p. 36). And so we have sought to make a Lab School education more responsive to the lives of our students. Their civics education begins with our community meetings and with the student judicial council where the bedrock values of democracy, respect for diverse opinions, and community responsibility are nurtured. Students complete independent projects each term rooted in their life interests: swimming, hiking, computers, a business enterprise. As we are able, academic course work is designed with the interests and experiences of students in mind. And students take as long as they need to master the material. "Follow the child," says Maria Montessori.

But we are not a progressive school in the strict sense that we adhere entirely to John Dewey's philosophy. And we are not a Montessori School either, as much as we feel a kinship with both approaches. So what are we? Who are we?

If we look at our program as a whole, it is in some respects quite traditional. We have a science curriculum with a prescribed scope and sequence. We have a humanities course which covers prescribed topics. Our second-language students memorize vocabulary words, our math groups are tracked, we give multiple-choice tests and assign grades. We sometimes give lectures, our students write academic essays, we use the MLA style sheet. And everybody takes the SAT.

So what gives? Are we progressive or are we traditional? Are we student centered or curriculum centered?

This is where my recent realization comes in. It has occurred to me during the last month or so that for two years we've been flip flopping between two different approaches. In working out some policies and issues, we have leaned toward the traditional, and with other policies and in other, bolder seasons, we have hammered out progressive solutions. How do we then address this inconsistency? We might say we need to just make up our minds about which approach to follow, and follow it. That appears to be the logical thing. But sometimes what appears logical on the surface isn't, and if we pause to think more penetratingly, I believe our reflections lead us elsewhere. I believe that all our flip flopping suggests that really we feel some allegiance to each philosophy and that the problem lies not in alternating between them, but rather in the haphazard manner in which we have done so. The solution then is not to artificially deny our attachment to one or the other, but rather to figure out how to more deliberately and creatively marry the two within our curriculum.

I would be denying something essential to my view of teaching if I determined that in the Lab School history course I ought to supply the students only with primary source documents, allow them to inquire into any aspect of history they wish and have them generate their knowledge of the past completely on their own. There is a certain cultural literacy that we owe to the next generation. History is a story, an ongoing narrative, and so the story should be told, the narrative conveyed.

At the same time, I would deny something equally essential if history class was simply a matter of telling stories for students to memorize. If that were the case, we would still be telling the lopsided story of Columbus the hero bringing civilization to the savage Indians in an untamed wilderness.

The point is that inquiry and narrative are both essential. Yes, it is better to teach a person *how* to fish, but it also helps if you give her a list of known fish in the lake, a current map of the surrounding geology, a few tips on where the fish have been biting, and maybe a slice of bread so she doesn't starve waiting for the first fish to strike.

Nowhere is the dilemma we face between progressive and traditional education more salient than with the notion of interdisciplinary studies. Mention the idea in a room full of teachers and they will commence waxing poetically about the connections between this and that in history and literature and math and science and helping students see the natural tie-ins among all those artificial subjects, etc. I think maybe I've been known to do that!

Well, we've been attempting just that in the Lab School for two years now, and I'm here to tell you it ain't so easy. What often ends up happening is that one discipline becomes dominant. If, say, we organize a unit of study around a science topic, the kids will get a lot of science, but the other disciplines end up getting marginalized. Maybe they do some algebra as it relates to the science equations. Perhaps they'll study a few famous scientists in connection with history, and they'll practice their writing skills in developing lab reports—all good things to be sure, but try to establish any kind of meaningful scope and sequence to a course as you march from unit to unit in this way and your students will rapidly become confused. On the other hand, it is important that our students make connections among different areas of study. It is important that they gain some sense of knowledge as a unified whole. How do we do this? We do it by respecting our allegiance to the disciplines and by exploiting opportunities for integration. We've done that to an extent already with the twenty- and forty-week exams, some joint projects in the humanities and science and math, but we need to do more and we need to do it more creatively and more deliberately. Figuring out how is our homework this summer.

As we enter our third year, we find ourselves facing several great paradoxes. We are traditional and we are progressive. We teach more by teaching less. We are student centered and we are curriculum centered. Robert Fulghum in his book *Maybe Maybe Not* writes about contradictions to live by: "Two heads are better than one" paired with "If you want something done right, then do it yourself." "He who hesitates is lost" paired with "Look before you leap." My favorite is one he had emblazoned on a tee shirt from his days as a teacher. The front of his shirt said, "Trust me, I'm a teacher." The back said, "Question authority."

If you find all of this flux and uncertainty unnerving, I would urge you to take heart. If we are questioning, thinking, and changing, then we are doing the very thing that all schools strive to teach: questioning, thinking, changing. I hope too that rather than being merely the passing characteristics of a new school that disappear as the school grows and matures, these remain permanent qualities of our collective endeavor, a trademark. As folks out there observe it, we will gain their respect. I am certain of it. It's happening already.

For example, look at the success of our senior class getting in to college. I can't resist reading the list again: University of New Hampshire, University of Montana, University of New Mexico, Rensselaer Polytechnic Institute, State University of New York at Albany, Plattsburgh, Oneonta, and Oswego, Syracuse College of Environmental Science and Forestry, New York University, Boston University, Berklee College of Music, Northeastern University, University of Massachusetts at Amherst, Warren Wilson College, Washington and Jefferson College, Alfred University, University of Minnesota, and Purdue.

Consider also the favorable attention we're getting in the papers and on TV. Here's a clip from Harry Rosenfeld, editor in chief of the *Times Union* who served on our Board of Examiners in January and wrote a commentary for the following Sunday paper. I quote, "The Lab School's inclusivity is its defining essence that should speak loudly to the rest of the world. Although everyone gets the chance to apply, all must meet the same set of standards, which the program makes clear are high. The relationships that emerge from students working shoulder to shoulder and meeting faculty on what appears to be more relaxed terms results in obvious accomplishments. For a moment being a part of the Lab School was instructive not only in witnessing what can be done in the real world with available means. It was also informative in substance." End quote.

Also, consider the growing list of those who have inquired and those who have visited the Lab School in its two short years: SUNY Albany Department of Atmospheric Sciences, Ravena Schools, Albany City Schools, Lake Luzerne Schools, Rensselaer Polytechnic Institute, The Annenberg Institute for School Reform, NYS Education Department, Union College, Russell Sage College, Capital Area School Development Association, The Lake George Schools, Shenendehowa Schools, The Parker School, Albany Academy, the New York State School Superintendents Association, The Boston Renaissance Charter School, the National Council for the Social Studies. The list goes on.

These are all conspicuous successes. More important, and much less observable, are the quiet victories fought for and won on a daily basis by our students working with their teachers, their peers, and their parents. Each time we do the oral exams, I am struck by the growth in confidence and speaking ability of so many individual students. The transformation is visible and it is real.

As we move into our third year and our second senior class, we will see wider acceptance still and a new year of growth and learning, and more, provocative contradictions. I am sure of it. Trust me, I'm a teacher.

# Afterword

What do you remember from high school? Do you remember all the presidents of the United States? Do you remember the titles of poems by William Wordsworth, William Blake, Andrew Marvell? Do you remember five geometry formulas? Can you recall the details of the Krebs cycle? Can you recite the conjugations of all regular verbs in Spanish? How many of the thousands of facts and concepts that you memorized in high school can you recall today? What percentage? Fifty percent? Twenty percent? Ten percent? Is it enough to justify four years of schooling, seven hours a day, five days a week, focusing primarily on the memorization of facts and concepts?

What do you remember from high school? Do you remember your friendships? A certain teacher who inspired you to work a little harder? A teacher who made you think? A project or two that was different from the usual porridge of school assignments and which, unlike most of your high school endeavors, you worked intently on?

We tend to forget most of the "content" of courses. What sticks are the opportunities (all too infrequent in conventional education) to engage deeply and interestedly with ideas and other people in ways that teach us how to think, how to communicate, how to be decent persons. We remember relationships—with persons and with ideas.

Ever since James Conant's study *The American High School Today* was released in 1959, Americans have increasingly come to believe in the virtues of the large, comprehensive high school. Today, its superiority is commonly assumed. It offers "something for everybody," and, we believe, it's scale offers us economy, too. But in this bargain we have lost something crucial. Courses alone do not make a school. Lots of courses do not make a great school. The value of a high school does not come from whether a student was able to take plant physiology, cultures of the Sahara, or advanced placement calculus in her junior year. Rather, the worth of a school may be measured by the extent to which its graduates can think adeptly and solve problems, communicate ably, demonstrate good citizenship, demonstrate maturity and confidence, and demonstrate some competence within a reasonable range of academic disciplines. Large high schools have given us lots of courses but they have broken down the sustained contact with people and ideas that gives an education sticking power.

In 1992, the Bethlehem School District chartered a new, "experimental" high school program carved out of the larger school system. The Lab School is small, personal, and demanding. Its students are extremely diverse and are voluntarily enrolled. The teachers have been granted a great deal of autonomy in crafting the educational program. And costs have been kept to the school district's per pupil allocation. The curriculum for the Lab School stresses the fundamentals of history, English, mathematics, science, and second language. Rather than offering a wide-ranging elective program, the Lab School stresses a deeper understanding of a more limited range of subjects. In so doing, teachers are able to link subjects together so that students can make connections between American history and American literature, for example, or chemistry and related math concepts. The idea is a trade-off. We have traded away the advantage of options that an elective-based program offers. But by scaling down and forcing a close working relationship among students and teachers (and parents), we have gained focus, intensity, and a strong sense of community.

The Lab School is small. Even after it grows to its full size, it will still involve only about a hundred students and a handful of teachers drawn from the major academic disciplines. Because it is small, Lab School students and teachers are able to build a strong sense of community. To the skeptic's ear, this may sound soft and vague, but it has direct academic payoff. When students feel a part of something, they care. When they care, they want to do their best. A frequent comment we hear from our students is, "I'm working harder, but I enjoy it." Community, decency, and rigor are the qualities that should most characterize a twenty-first century school because they are the qualities our society most urgently needs. And they are the primary goals of the Lab School. Until the Lab School, I never realized what a potent ally the sort of esprit de corps that we enjoy could be for teachers battling the general malaise of student apathy.

The Lab School is committed to operating at prevailing school district costs. While my own firm conviction is that American society must make a substantially greater financial commitment to its schools, the Lab School is an effort to see what can be done by reallocating existing resources as opposed to adding new money. Like all other public schools, we struggle against scarcity of resources.

The Lab School is not an "alternative" school intended for students who are not able to function in a standard program. Instead, the Lab School is open to all students who are attracted to its distinctive features. Our current student body represents a cross section of the larger high school. Some of our students are already involved in college-level work. Others, we project, may need an additional semester or year to complete the program. In dealing with such a diverse group, I have found that the greatest academic difference among students lies not in "innate intelligence" but in confidence and self-discipline. I am convinced that very nearly all students can perform to a high level if we insist on nothing less. As a corollary, I have found that all students are gifted. Their gifts vary: verbal ability, mathematical ability, artistic talent, leadership qualities, organizational skill, a calm spirit, humility, humor, compassion, diligence. The list goes on. All these gifts are valuable to society, and all should be acknowledged and nurtured. Why some of our schools tout "gifted" programs that recognize only a narrow range of talents—corresponding with quantitative and analytic ability (and parental clout)—is unfortunate. We need to encourage in our schools those other qualities as well—artistry, diligence, self-discipline, compassion, humility, leadership, and many others.

Some students require special attention, but working more closely with students in general in the Lab School, I find that only some of the time are these the students who are identified as "handicapped" or "gifted." I can think of a handful of students I am working with right now who have taken up probably two to three times the amount of attention we give to our students generally in the form of after-school help, parent conferences, disciplinary action, counseling, and personal reflection, but who have never been and probably never will be identified as handicapped or gifted. Their challenges elude bureaucratic detection but are immediately apparent to a group of teachers with the opportunity to get to know their students. One of the great rewards of the Lab School has been the opportunity to work intensively with a small group of colleagues in the service of a relatively small group of students whom we get to know well.

We are a real school with real problems, and we don't hide them. We face all the challenges of any public school program: drugs, alcohol abuse, discipline, you name it. But we address our problems squarely and publicly. I believe that in this respect we can serve students better than a large school. Because we're small, problems get noticed. (Our students say, "You can't hide in Lab School!") We've intervened and made a difference already in this area. All schools face challenges. A good school acknowledges them and wrestles with them.

Parental choice and school autonomy have been key factors in our program's development. Because our students and their parents chose the Lab School, they come in with a positive attitude. Because they can also choose to leave (though there are practical difficulties in doing so), we (the teachers) are motivated to make the program the best we can. We have a real stake in our little school's success.

Along with parental choice, school autonomy has played an important role. Cut loose from the conventional program, we have been free to devise new policies and curricula. (Alternatively stated: we have been under enormous pressure to do same!) Our freedom has engendered much discourse among Lab School teachers, students, and parents. What is the best way to report student progress? What should our standards be? How should we present our students to colleges? What is meaningful assessment? We have questioned much. We have disagreed. We have faced good times and hard times, and we have labored to work things out because we have to. Regular, lively discourse among all of the primary constituents of a school (students, parents, and teachers) about what their school should be, ought to go on in every school. It happens in the Lab School because we must chart our own course. What if every school had to chart its own course?

Should the Lab School serve as a model for others to replicate? Good schools are never replicated. They are not based on models to be "plugged in." They emerge from discourse and problem solving at the local level. The Lab School was designed by local people and crafted to suit the circumstances and needs of our own community. While we benefited from visits to other schools and read much about school reform, we remained intellectually in charge. A good school is not just the curriculum and philosophy, it is also the present and past relationships of its constituents. And that is not replicable.

After thirteen years in public education, I am finally teaching in the kind of school I have always dreamed about. I am lucky that I work in a school district where the teachers, administrators, and school board recognize the value of trying something new and have the courage to make it happen. I am especially grateful to the Bethlehem High School faculty. Although we are philosophically a divergent group of people—some colleagues will argue vehemently the merits of the conventional program—we respect the desire of colleagues to try out different approaches.

Even under the very favorable circumstances we have faced, it took us five years to get the Lab School launched. I know there are many educators out there who are not as lucky as I am. They long to enact *their* vision of The Good School, but the obstacles are too great. At a time when so many readily acknowledge an urgent need to try out different approaches in public education, why does it continue to be so difficult?

# Appendix A
## College Admissions for Lab School Seniors, 1996

Bryn Mawr (two students)

Rensselaer Polytechnic Institute

University of Rochester (early decision)

Skidmore

Rochester Institute of Technology

Alfred University (two students, two presidential scholarships)

Lafayette University (two students)

SUNY Geneseo (two students)

St. Lawrence University (with scholarship)

Clarkson (early decision)

University of Delaware (honors program)

Bard College

Union College (three students)

Worcester Polytechnic Institute

Binghamton University (three students)

University of Connecticut

Green Mountain College

Lyndon State College

University of Texas

Hobart College

Eugene Lang College

University of Vermont

Muhlenberg College

Dickinson College

SUNY Cortland

George Washington University (two students)

Alvernia College

West Virginia Wesleyan

University of New Hampshire

SUNY Plattsburg
University of North Carolina at Wilmington
University of Massachusetts at Amherst
SUNY Oneonta
SUNY Buffalo
Ithaca College
Grove City College
Quinnipiac College (with scholarship)
Western State University
College of Saint Rose
University of Maine
University of Rhode Island
Hartwick College

# Appendix B

*philosophy & history*

The Bethlehem Central Lab School is a small, rigorous high school program carved out of the larger Bethlehem Central High School in which it is physically situated. Designed by Bethlehem Central faculty and community members committed to excellence through innovation, the Lab School represents a bold educational thrust into the 21st century. Lab School students and faculty alike have been characterized as a community of risktakers, pioneering active modes of learning that frequently involve students in independent research, formal presentations and interdisciplinary projects—all in a context of demanding coursework.

a high school program
of Bethlehem Central School District

*excellence through innovation*

A SCHOOL WITHIN A SCHOOL:
The Lab School is a small
high school program
carved out of the larger
Bethlehem Central High School
in which it is physically situated
and from which it draws
its students at the completion
of their freshman year.
The Bethlehem community
is a suburb of Albany,
New York State's capital.
Approximately 88%
of BCHS graduates continue
their education beyond
high school, with the majority
attending four-year colleges.

Chartered in 1992 as a local response to calls from business, government and education to experiment with new methods of teaching and learning, the Lab School—while still in its infancy—has attracted widespread attention for its success in bringing innovative approaches to public education. The Lab School has been featured in the local press, as well as in national professional journals. Lab School teachers are frequent presenters at professional conferences, and visitors to the Lab School from other school districts are a common sight.

The Lab School is small and will remain so, size being one of its defining characteristics. The Lab School is committed to innovation as an ongoing endeavor. Student governance is a major focus of the Lab School as well, based on the premise that the best preparation for citizenship is practice with citizenship responsibilities in school. The Lab School is also committed to employing to the greatest extent possible "real world" forms of assessment. Thus, oral presentations, written research, portfolios and student internships are all a regular part of student life in the Lab School.

*student body*

Admission to Lab School is open to all students who attend Bethlehem Central High School. The decision to enroll in Lab School is made during the freshman year and commences with the sophomore year.

Layout design of "Lab School, Who We Are" by Kristi Carr, formerly of the Bethlehem School District

203

The student remains in Lab School until graduation. Thus Lab School represents an alternative high school choice from a student's sophomore year through graduation.

Historically, the Lab School has attracted a full range of students in terms of ability, interests and scholastic achievement. It is a very diverse student body! Nonetheless, Lab School holds every student to the same high standard of achievement. For some students this means extensive additional coursework during summer months plus the possibility of an additional semester or year in order to reach the Lab School's graduation standards. For a few students, it is possible to consider graduating a semester earlier than is customary. In the event that Lab School enrollment is oversubscribed, a lottery determines admission.

## curriculum

Every Lab School graduate completes four years of math, science, history, English and a second language. In addition, the Lab School curriculum demands independent research, a rigorous examination process employing outside evaluators and a senior project/internship. The Lab School also involves students in an elective program and a system of student governance.

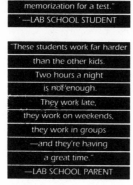

"I feel I learn how to apply my skills instead of just memorization for a test."
—LAB SCHOOL STUDENT

"These students work far harder than the other kids. Two hours a night is not enough. They work late, they work on weekends, they work in groups —and they're having a great time."
—LAB SCHOOL PARENT

**SMART**
**science, math**
**& related technologies**

In developing the science portion of the Lab School's curriculum, teachers solicited input from the science departments at Rensselaer Polytechnic Institute. With RPI's help in selecting essential content, a rigorous two-year sequence in biology and chemistry has been created, as well as a third year of selected units that integrate physics and math in a semester course. Combined with an earth science course completed in the freshman year, the Lab School science program provides every graduate with a solid and well-rounded science background.

The SMART math sequence begins with an integrated approach to topics in geometry (NYS Course II), building on the algebra coursework (Course I) that students complete before entering Lab School. From there, students continue with trigonometry (Course III), with continual stress on mastery of algebra skills. The overarching goal of the math program is for students to attain an understanding of the three basic foundations of high school mathematics (algebra, geometry, trigonometry), using the foundations to develop their analytical and problem-solving skills through projects that link with science and technology. In addition, students are exposed to number theory, probability, statistical theory and other pre-calculus topics. Some students continue their studies through calculus. All students gain extensive experience with the graphing calculator (TI-82).

**humanities**

The Lab School humanities program combines content traditionally studied in college prep courses in English and history. Using a cross-disciplinary approach, every student completes a one-year course in American studies and a one-year course in Western and Middle Eastern studies. A third year exposes students to special topics in the humanities that change from year to year. Combined with a student's freshman year high school coursework in world literature and global studies, every Lab School graduate leaves the program with a solid four-year grounding in the humanities. Humanities coursework in the Lab School includes an Advanced Placement exam option in European history, U.S. history, English language and composition and English language and literature.

### second language/second culture

All Lab School students are required to attend second language/second culture class for the duration of their Lab School experience. This commitment ensures that, upon graduation, every student will have completed at least four years of second language instruction and achieved, at the least, modest proficiency and, for some, substantial fluency.

### elective courses

Every Lab School student completes at least two years of study in an elective area, choosing among music, fine arts or occupational education.

### senior project/internship

During the senior year, a Lab School student designs and executes a culminating project of major scope. Projects —which generally include a major off-campus component—are carefully supervised and scrutinized to ensure that they are of the highest standard and provide a bridge to the student's post-high school experiences.

### portfolio projects

In addition to coursework, students are regularly engaged in "portfolio projects." A portfolio project is a student-designed activity in which the student crafts a personal interest into an academic assignment. Some recent examples include a winter camping experience, the development of a computerized billing program for a summer lawn care business, modification of a desktop computer (including installation of a new motherboard, hard drive and internal modem) and community service at a local soup kitchen. Each portfolio project is based on a contract worked out in advance and specifying the graduation goals that the project will satisfy, a timeline for completion and description of a substantial product to be submitted for evaluation.

### student governance

The Lab School takes seriously its mission to prepare students for participation in a democratic society. Therefore, several periods each week are devoted to the Lab School's program of student governance. Once each week, students and teachers assemble as a community for discussion and resolution of school-wide issues. The meeting is student-run and decisions are reached by consensus or vote. Another period is set aside each week for students to meet in small groups with a teacher/advisor to establish the agenda for the weekly community meeting.

### special programs

The Lab School regularly sets aside Wednesday afternoon for special programs. Any academically valuable event that does not fit neatly into a regular class period is fair game for Wednesday afternoon. Special programs include field trips to cultural or scientific locations, guest speakers, student presentations, movies, plays, concerts, community service and more.

## *evaluation*

### teacher-assigned grades

For coursework and portfolio projects, students are scored numerically by their teachers. (See transcript for description of scoring system.)

### narrative evaluation

Every Lab School graduate receives a summary narrative evaluation by each of his or her teachers and guidance counselor. **It is important to note that evaluators are not selected by the student; rather, each teacher completes a narrative evaluation on every student to ensure a full and frank assessment.**

## major presentations

Every semester, each Lab School student develops a major research paper related to coursework, prepares an oral presentation of research findings, and reads critically the research of selected classmates. At the end of each semester—to ensure student achievement is measured by a demanding "real world" standard—students present their research in small groups before a Board of Examiners that includes prominent citizens drawn from the Albany community and beyond, as well as Lab School teachers.

A partial listing of examiners during the 1993-95 school years includes:

Geoffrey Gould, Director of Undergraduate Admissions, Binghamton University

Jeanne Jenkins, Acting Dean of Admissions, Rensselaer Polytechnic Institute

Dr. Gary Wnek, Chairman, Chemistry Dept., Rensselaer Polytechnic Institute

Diane Crozier, Associate Dean of Admissions, Union College

James Bennett, PhD, Principal Technologist, General Electric, Selkirk, NY

John Faso, New York State Assemblyman, 102nd District

Harold S. Williams, President, The Rensselaerville Institute

Gregory Nash, President, National Education Association of New York

William Collins, President, Bethlehem Central Board of Education

Leslie Loomis, Superintendent, Bethlehem Central School District

Harry Rosenfeld, Editor, Times Union Newspaper

## *Lab School faculty*

**Michele Atallah**
**Second Language/Second Culture**
B.A., University at Albany; M.A., University at Albany
Lebansese-born and fluent in French, Spanish, Arabic and English, Ms. Atallah directs a student-centered class in which the emphasis is on language fluency and cross-cultural understanding. Through the regular use of interactive software, satellite TV foreign language programming and linguistic/cultural immersion activities, Ms. Atallah's students learn through doing.

**Patricia Baran**
**Science, Math and Related Technologies**
B.A. and M.A., State University at Albany
Ms. Baran brings to the Lab School the newest ideas from higher education in teaching math to sutdents of all ability levels. Ms. Baran holds all lab school students to a high level of math competence.

**Jane Feldmann**
**Science, Math and Related Technologies**
B.A., Syracuse University; M.A., Syracuse University
On Ms. Feldmann's initiative, the Lab School has joined in a partnership with Rensselaer Polytechnic Institute in the design of the Lab School science program. In addition to her work with the Lab School, Ms. Feldmann is a frequent presenter for science and education conferences.

**James Nehring**
**Humanities**
B.A., University of Virginia; M.A.T., Brown University
Author of books and articles on education, Mr. Nehring leads the history portion of the Lab School's interdisciplinary humanities curriculum. He is a frequent presenter at conferences and appears on radio and TV. His books include **The Schools We Have, the Schools We Want** (Jossey-Bass, 1992) and **Why Do We Gotta Do This Stuff, Mr. Nehring?** (M. Evans, 1989). His work has appeared in the Washington **Post**, the Chicago **Tribune**, **Education Week**, **Social Science Record** and elsewhere.

**William Wojcik**
**Humanities**
B.A., SUNY New Paltz; M.A.T., Union College
Mr. Wojcik became interested in teaching as a result of working as a tutor at the New Paltz Campus Writing Center. He entered the profession through Union's innovative master's program, which is closely aligned in both philosophy and practice with the Lab School. A participant in the Capital District Writing Project and the National Research Center for Literature Teaching and Learning, Mr. Wojcik is an enthusiastic teacher and student of all aspects of English and the humanities.

**Visiting teachers**
**Music, Fine Arts, Occupational Education**
In addition to its permanent faculty, the Lab School benefits from the participation of various Bethlehem Central High School teachers who serve for usually a year as "visiting teachers," directing the Lab School's elective program.

# Appendix C

*Please note: This transcript is designed with the time constraints of college admissions officers well in mind. At the same time it seeks to provide a thorough and rich evaluation of student progress. To those ends, Part I offers an overview of student achievement at a glance, while Parts II and III provide more in-depth exploration and substantiation of student achievement.*

## Bethlehem Laboratory High School Student Transcript

Student:                     Date: 10/95
Expected Date of Graduation: June, 1996

### EXPLANATION OF TRANSCRIPT

To earn a Lab School diploma, the student must demonstrate proficiency as a/an

A) adept thinker and problem solver
B) capable and committed citizen
C) able communicator
D) confident and mature individual
E) competent scholar in a range of academic disciplines

Students develop proficiency in these areas through course work, portfolio projects, major presentations, and the senior project/internship. (See Lab School Program Folder for a full description.) Tonindicate proficiency, the Lab School emplys the following grading scale.

6 = special commendation; work of exceptional quality; awarded to fewer than one percent of assignments
5 = distinguished achievement; equivalent to 90–100 in a rigorous, college-preparatory high school course
*4 = mastery; equivalent to 80–89 in a rigorous, college-preparatory high school course
3 = approaching mastery, remediation recommended
2 = insufficient progress
1 = seriously deficient
0 = work of little or no merit

*N.B.: student must achieve a level of at least "4" in *all* goal areas inorder to earn the diploma.

This report shows progress to date toward graduation. It is divided into three parts.

Part I:    summary of progress toward graduation goals
Part II    collection of narrative evaluations by teachers and guidance counselor
Part III:  representative selection of student's work submitted in support of graduation goals

# Part I
## Summary of Progress Toward Graduation Goals

Student Name:            Student ID #

**Goal A: adept thinker and problem solver**    SP
1. Think logically and creatively
2. Apply reasoning skills to issues and problems
3. Use current and developing technologies
4. Use libraries and other resources for information skills
5. Use reasoning skills to solve societal problems

**Goal B: capable and committed citizen**    SP
1. Effectively apply knowledge of political, social, and economic processes:
   a. at local and state levels
   b. at ntional and international levels
2. Understand adult roles of
   a. parent, home manager, family member
   b. worker
   c. learner
   d. consumer
   e. citizen
3. Demonstrate a commitment to justice, honesty, and democratic values
4. Respect and cooperate with persons of different race, sex, ability, culture
5. Respect the natural environment
6. Required activity: 15 hours of community service

**Goal C: able communicator**    SP
1. Comprehend written, spoken, and visual presentations in various media

2. Express English clearly through
    a. speaking
    b. listening
    c. reading
    d. writing
3. Exercise aesthetic judgment
4. Required activity: Senior Presentation

**Goal D: confident and mature individual**     SP
1. Possess self-esteem
2. maintain physical, mental, and emotional health
3. Understand ill effects of alcohol, tobacco, other drugs, and other practices dangerous to health
4. Demonstrate ability to set and achieve goals
5. Required activity: senior internship/project

**Goal E: competent scholar in a range of academic disciplines**
*Science/Math and Related Technologies*
Environmental Chemistry     4+
Principles in Biology     4+
Principles of Geometry     4
Linear Functions     4+

*Second Language/Second Culture*
Spanish III     4
Spanish IV     4

*Humanities*
American Studies     4+
Western and Mideastern Studies     4+
Senior Seminar (Great Works)     SP

*Elective Courses*
Marketing     75

*Mid-year and End-of-Year Presentations*
January 94     4+
June 94     4+
January 95     4+
June 95     4+

**Academic Honors**
Outstanding Research Report, June 1995

**M** indicates Master
**SP** indicates Satisfactory progress but not completed

# Part II
## *Narrative Evaluation*

This section of the transcript includes narrative evaluations written by each of the students' Lab School teachers.

Please note: This student has not exercised any choice as to who writes the narrative evaluations. Rather, each of his or her regular Lab School teachers has written an evaluation in order to ensure that assessment is broad, thorough, and uncompromising.

These are frank narrative evaluations (NOT standard letters of recommendation) and should be viewed in that light.

### Teacher Narrative Evaluations of John Doe 10/95

*Teacher: Jane Feldmann*
*Subject: Science, Math, and Related Technologies*
When I think of evaluating John I think of a student with a high degree of honesty and integrity, as well as good academic ability. John has natural leadership ability and is not afraid to express his feelings and opinions. As John has matured over the course of the past three years, he has grown in his interpersonal skills and is using this leadership ability more effectively. As a student of science I have found John to be a good thinker and problem solver. He could be an excellent student in science, not just a good one. I would like to see him set his goals higher and achieve to his fullest capacity.

*Teacher: William Wojcik*
*Subject: Humanities*
John is a well-informed student, able to add relevant comments and observations to discussions on a wide variety of topics. He is able to approach these topics with both a serious intellect and a striking sense of humor, although occasionally through both sides he reveals an impatience with the direction or content of the discussion. His work habits are good; he rarely turns in a late assignment. Within the realm of language arts, John has made his biggest impression as an oral communicator, especially when given the freedom to explore and report on a topic of his own choice.

*Teacher: Patricia Baran*
*Subject: Science, Math, and Related Technologies*
John took the initiative to advance in math by taking a class over the summer. In class John would often question "why." He did not only want to

know how things were done but why. I feel John's inquisitive nature, especially in math, is a positive attribute.

Many times John would do average work when capable of doing very well, He needs to focus on setting higher standards for himself.

*Teacher: James Nehring*
*Subject: Humanities*
In the three years I have worked with John, he has consistently demonstrated a high level of competence in writing, class discussion, and critical reading. He has been in general very diligent in his studies and a leader among his peers who is willing to speak his mind quietly and earnestly especially wen it goes against the mainstream. John is able to quickly grasp the subtleties that surround complex issues. He uses his wonderful sense of humor to break the ice in social situations and is mindful to include those who appear excluded.

*Teacher: Michele Atallah*
*Subject: Second Language/Second Culture*
I have known John for three years in the Lab School and through my Spanish classes. John has maintained a passing grade even though Spanish is not his favorite subject. But as part of the Lab School team I have the opportunity to see John in a variety of situations.

John works very hard and succeeds in difficult situations. He is charismatic, assertive and a well-rounded person. He constantly seeks intellectual challenges and is an active member of the Lab School community, sharing his ideas and opinions. John has learned to work efficiently and effectively with others on team projects. He is a very conscientious student with perfect school attendance.

John is ready to attend university and will do very well. I believe John will be an asset to your program and thrive in a university setting.

# Part III
## *Representative Work by the Student*

This portion of the transcript is a sampling of student work offered in support of scores and narratives in Parts I and II.

Student Name:
Subject Teacher: Ms. Feldmann
Date Completed: January 1994
Grade Received: 5+

*Topic/Description:* "The Environmental Conspiracy." The information presented to us about our environment is often one-sided. This is due, in part, to influence of the media and the environmental special-interest groups. In this paper, I demonstrate that there is often another side to stories of environmental doom.

*Selection Rationale:* The paper shows my ability to fairly show both sides of an issue, as well as forming an opinion. It also shows my ability to form a conclusion and back it up with researched facts.

## The Environmental Conspiracy

We have been manipulated and deceived. Facts have been distorted and exaggerations have been made as to the state of our planet. The truth is there is no conclusive evidence to support the claim that the world's environment is in great peril from the activities of mankind. I will deal with two issues in this report, one regional and one global, state my opinions, and back them up with facts. I will also show a truly worthy issue that has not been given enough attention.

We have all read about the controversy of global warming and the Greenhouse Effect. When Ultra-Violet rays from the sun bounce off the Earth, some are held in by the gases in our atmosphere, mainly Carbon Dioxide. This process is the main reason that our planet stays at a life-sustaining temperature. Many environmentalists and scientists claim that human activities have dangerously increased the levels of CO to the point where our planet is in serious danger of becoming too hot. They point to auto emissions and factory smokestack discharges as being the primary culprits (8). They have conducted research which suggests that the overall global temperature has increased (6). If it increases too much, it will result in flooding, more hurricanes, and huge changes in our weather patterns (8). Environmentalists claim drastic actions to curb releasing these gases is needed to protect future generations from environmental apocalypse. In response to the argument that we should wait until better research is done, many ecologists say that the small steps necessary to secure environmental stability are far less complex and harmful than the alternatives left to us if we take no action and allow the problem to get even more out of control.

That is not a rational argument. The planet has been around for five billion years. We have been keeping accurate weather records needed for good, reliable research for at best, 50 years (7). To "cry fire" at only 50 years of work is foolish, especially when action against this "problem" would be very costly to technology and industry. Earth has experienced thousands of long- and short-term weather patterns. Perhaps the most dramatic examples of this that we know were the ice ages. During the last period, 14,000 years ago, ice extended all the way down to present-day Chicago in the Western Hemisphere (2). There are always short-term and long-term changes in our global weather patterns and people, crops, and nature have always adapted to short- and long-term swings (5). One example is the last ice age 14,000 years ago, where people survived all over the world (2). People aren't creating these changes, it is our planet working and evolving.

There is a great deal of diversity in the opinions of scientists. Contrary to what some may believe, many environmental scientists are very uncertain that the temperature will rise due to the greenhouse effect and human activities. A recent poll conducted by the International Panel on Climate Change (IPCC) had some interesting results. The IPCC found that up to one-half of the scientists polled did not believe in the IPCC estimate of .3 degrees celsius temperature rise per decade because of human activity (6). These scientists attributed any growth to natural climate changes. The other half did believe that the threat of global warming existed and they suggested action. However, this is an issue where any "preventative" action would be costly and time consuming. I feel that it is wise to have a large majority of scientists advocating such action.

There is also very confusing data as to how much our planet has heated up, or if it has heated up at all. Of what we know of global warming, the first and worst temperature changes will occur at the poles. Early in j1993, U.S. scientists were able to study Russian documents from their bases on the north pole. This data charted the temperature changes in the arctic. The results were very surprising (7). Jonathan D. Kahl, a climatologist at the University of Wisconsin, puts it this way, "The predicted widespread warming was not observed" (7).

We must also consider the fact that even using the best equipment and evidence available, scientists have constantly given bad predictions. Wise men would "interpret" the future in flocks of geese, in the guts of animals, and in tea leaves (10). Those were considered accurate methods of forecasting back then just as computers are today. Today, we all know that the entrails of a goat do not provide a very accurate look into the future. As recently as the 1970s, scientists were warning of global cooling being a major threat (5). It is not wise, no matter how emotionally people tell it to you, to rush into drastic action with too little research. According to James Elsner of Florida State University, "It's impossible to tell whether the long-term warming results from a natural fluctuation in the climate or from the greenhouse gases accumulating in the atmosphere" (4).

Dixie Lee Ray, the former governor of the state of Washington, assesses the situation this way: She says that it is very arrogant of people to assume that they have that much power over nature. Weather changes, patterns change, and this is vastly beyond people's control (3). The movement by some to call this issue a crisis created by human stupidity and promote to immediate and drastic action is both illogical and foolish.

I think many people are forgetting the incredible power of nature. Nature in some form created this world, and nature can and is changing it. Mother Nature can level a city it took people hundreds of years to create in six seconds. Nature can destroy millions of years of erosion and slow change instantly by an earthquake or tidal wave. Nature can slowly create wonderful living creatures out of the most basic of substances. Also, I believe nature is powerful enough to adapt to the changes to our planet.

Another example of exaggeration by the media deals with logging in the Northwest, specifically the state of Oregon. Environmentalists claim that the logging industry is destroying the fragile environment of the rare spotted owl. The owl, they say, would be an indicator species of serious ecological trouble and it must be protected. Many say the companies have no environmental responsibility and that they only care about the bottom line, their profit. They will make a buck no matter what the risk to the forest or the creatures living in it.

There is, of course, another side to this story. I don't believe that the environmentalists mentioned the fact that the owls do not live exclusively in the areas being logged. They live in southern California, in the forests of the Puget Sound Lowlands, and up into British Columbia (1). The spotted owl is in no danger of having vast areas of its territory destroyed. The creatures of nature have a fantastic ability to adapt and find new homes. A forest is also not destroyed by logging. The logging industry does not cut down every tree and leave the former forest a vast wasteland of stumps like many anti-logging advocates would like us to believe. Legitimate companies have a system of harvesting only a certain number of trees in a given area. The land is still green even in areas that are heavily logged.

There is also the matter of the economy to consider. Many towns have been built around logging mills. Most of the people living here work for the lumber industry. If logging were to stop, the economy of all the towns would be severely depressed. The town would possibly not have enough money for proper police, fire and ambulance, schools, or other public programs. The state would also suffer because the tax base would be reduced and they would have to spend more money helping these depressed towns deal with the leaving of the industry. Would the laying off of the thousands of workers employed by the logging industry in that region be worth the complete protection of these woods? Would the overall impact, however small, on all businesses that use wood be justified? Would other sites be more heavily cut to make up for the losses? Would new sites have to be found and logged for new sources of lumber? It would be important to listen to the little girl who could say "Since they closed the mill, my Daddy doesn't have a job and I have no new clothes for my under-funded school." In my opinion, these opinions illustrate the many good reasons to continue logging in the Northwest.

The biggest player in the game of ecological exaggeration is the media. There is an old journalistic saying "No problem, no news," and the media constantly hypes up problems for ratings (10). We must keep in mind that no matter how good the intentions, environmentalists and the media also have their own self-interests in mind, and they have no problems with putting their "spin" on the issues. A prime example of the media overplay of the environment is as follows (10):

1.    February 1992, NASA warns of developing hole in the ozone layer over the United States. This prompts environmental action by Congress and President Bush to push up the deadline for the end of CFCs in the U.S., from the year 2000 to 1995.

2.    In their February 17th issue, *Time* magazine responds to NASA by making the news their front-page article.

3.    On April 30th, NASA holds a news conference to announce that the ozone hole had been "averted." In their May 11th issue, *Time* posts a *4-line mention* of the news and fail to mention that their front-page article had been based on faulty and presumptuous research.

This example not only shows science's interest to propel fears of environmental doom, but it also shows the media's eagerness to respond to any news with hyped-up announcements.

All these points I have made in this paper do not condone nor advocate waste. There are certainly instances where the environment has been grossly mistreated. In British Columbia, mining companies did not properly deal with their waste chemicals used in mining for minerals. These highly toxic chemicals leaked into the streams and destroyed huge amounts of salmon eggs, severely depleting their genetic stock of the region (3). This is an example of gross negligence and disrespect for our world and things like that must be stopped because there is never a reason for wanton destruction and waste. My point is that there are many productive and wonderful ways we can use our beautiful planet. Fishing, logging, trapping, hunting, manufacturing, offshore drilling, damming, mining, and, in some cases, whaling all greatly benefit people in so many ways.

I am also not saying that Earth is free from problems. A semi-environmental issue, over-population, is very serious. Population has grown slowly since people's beginning. It took till 1776 to reach 1 billion on the entire planet. It took till World War II to have two billion people. And in less than

50 years, three billion new babies have been born. At 5.5–5.6 billion today, it is expected that population will reach 9 billion by 2035 (9). This is a problem that, unlike some, has thousands of years of information to support it. How much media attention has it been given compared to environmental issues?

As you can see, there is a great deal of diversity of issues and opinions. Many smart people have spent time researching and thinking about these complex issues. Only time will tell the wisdom of the varying viewpoints but diversity is always good on any issues where the best-educated choice can be made.

In concluding, I strongly believe that there are many more important problems we should be facing as a nation and as a world. The economy, poverty and hunger, and world over-population are all urgent and pressing. I feel many people have been distorting our perceptions and manipulating our emotions to put the environment on the main agenda. It is time that we take a step back, and objectively and without prejudices look at our more important problems and how we as a world can deal with them.

### Bibliography

1. *World Book Encyclopedia*, 1992: volume 14.

2. *Alaska* by James Michener, copyright 1988 by Ballantine Books.

3. Questions answered by Andrew Miner about Dixie Lee Ray and the Salmon kill in Canada.

4. Article on page 95 of *Science News* from August 10, 1991: *"Discrepancies in Global Warming Data."*

5. Article on page 6 of *The Christian Science Monitor* from May 21, 1992: *"A Different View of Global Warming."*

6. Article on page 365 of *Science Times* from May 30, 1992: *"Climate Change: A Diversity of Views."*

7. Article on page 96 of *Business Week* from February 8, 1993: *"Predictions about Global Warming May Cool off a Bit."*

8. Article from *The Christian Science Monitor* from June 10, 1992: *"Let's Be Sensible about Global Warming."*

9. *Earth in the Balance* by Al Gore, copyright 1992 by Houghton Mifflin Company.

10. *Eco-Scam: The False Prophets of Ecological Apocalypse*, copyright 1993 by St. Martin's Press.

# *Appendix D*

Volume I, Issue 1                                                                 August, 1993

# FUTURES

Newsletter of the Bethlehem Laboratory High School, Delmar, NY

## Read This First...

We're launched! As September approaches, we anticipate a program characterized by high academic standards, strong support for individual students, and creativity as both a goal for students and a guiding principle in the development of curriculum. In short, our aim (and our motto) is excellence through innovation.

This issue of FUTURES brings both news and instructions that you will need to act on right away. Please read the issue carefully. Please note also the two enclosures. One is your schedule for the 1993-94 school year. The other is a field trip permission slip that you will need to mail along with a check. Please see the related articles in this issue for both of these items.

A word about our newsletter. "Futures" implies several ideas. First, is the future-orientation of the Lab School which seeks to prepare students for life in the next century (now looming imminently!). Second is the anticipation that new ways of teaching students well, pioneered here in the Lab School will catch on and spread. Finally, and most importantly, are the futures of our students, your children, who have been entrusted to our care-- a responsibility we take most seriously.

May we all-- students, parents, teachers-- join together in a fruitful collaboration and a successful first year. Onward!

Sincerely,

James Nehring, Humanities Teacher
Michele Atallah, Integrated Arts Teacher
Jane Feldmann, Sciences Teacher
Susan Terrell, Sciences Teacher (math)

Lab School Theme for 1993-94:

Diversity: weakness or strength?

## Your Schedule

In the mailing that brings you this issue of FUTURES you should find your schedule for the 1993-94 school year. You have been assigned to either the "Blue" section or the "Green" section. Blue/green section assignments are driven largely by student choice of a second language as well as a desire to achieve a mix of boys and girls and tenth and eleventh graders. The section assignment in no way reflects anyone's estimation of student ability or talent. Furthermore, sectioning applies to your academic classes (humanities, sciences, integrated arts) only. During the "Community Meeting" and "Weekly Program," students in both blue and green sections will come together. Also, the blue/green sectioning does not apply to your advisory group. You will be assigned to one of three advisory groups in September.

If you have signed up for a music group, this should appear on your schedule. If it does not, or if it is incorrect, please contact the school at once (439-4921) and leave a message for any one of the Lab School teachers. Do likewise if there is any other sort of problem with your schedule.

Please note also that periods three and four are the "Project Blocks." During this time Lab School students will meet with visiting teachers. The visiting teachers for 1993-94 are as follows: Diane Segal (art), Frank Leavitt (music), Angela Guptill (occupational ed.), and rotating faculty (physical education).

You will receive a copy of your schedule with room assignments by the first day of school.

### Academic Skills Mini-course Planned

In order to lay a solid foundation for the school year, all Lab School students will take part in a one day mini-course during the second week focusing on academic skills. The course will include segments on time management, notetaking techniques, group study skills, accessing information resources and more. The mini-course will extend work begun during the orientation field trip of September 13 and 14. (See related story, page 2.) The course will be held on Wednesday, Sept. 15 and Friday, Sept. 17.

217

# Math Teacher Appointed

The Lab School is thrilled to announce the appointment of Susan Terrell as math teacher. Ms. Terrell, who holds degrees from SUNY Binghamton (Master of Science in Teaching) and SUNY Geneseo (Bachelor of Arts in Mathematics) comes to Bethlehem from a tenured position in the Norwich (NY) City School District. In addition to strong credentials in mathematics, Ms. Terrell possesses a background in computers having taught the Advanced Placement Pascal course at Norwich.

Ms. Terrell will join Jane Feldmann in teaching the Lab School's "sciences" curriclulum, a course that integrates mathematics, science and technology. In addition to her responsibilities in the Lab School, Ms. Terrell will teach two math classes in the High School.

## Many Thanks...

THANK YOU to The Tri-Village Welcome Wagon for their generous donation of $125 to the Lab School. While the Lab School is committed to operating at current School District spending levels, there are numerous start-up costs that we must meet. The Welcome Wagon's donation is a welcome relief. Thank you again.

THANK YOU to the DiMaggio family for their generous donation of a sofa and chair for our community room.

THANK YOU to the Hedges family for their generous donation of a Zenith (IBM compatible) computer.

## Do It Now!

Checklist of important items:

*Notify High School (439-4921) of any problem with your schedule.

*Mark Monday Sept. 13 and Tuesday, Sept. 14 on your calendar now for the Lab School Orientation Field trip.

*Mail signed Field Trip Permission form with check for $55 (payable to Bethlehem Central Schools) to:
  Michele Atallah
  Bethlehem High School
  700 Delaware Avenue
  Delmar, NY  12054
*Plan to bring sleeping bag/bed roll, personal items, and towel on field trip

# Overnight Field Trip Planned

All Lab School students will attend an overnight Lab School orientation field trip from Monday, September 13 to Tuesday, September 14. The purpose of this trip is to begin to build team skills and familiarize students with a number of Lab School programs. Representatives from the Albany County Substance Abuse Prevention Program, experienced in developing team skills with adult and student groups in business and school settings, will lead several team training workshops. Workshops conducted by Lab School teachers will also be held in such areas as academic skills and student governance.

Skills developed during the field trip workshops will be extended in regular Lab School classes. Additionally, a five hour mini-course in study skills and time management will be conducted for all Lab School students on the Wednesday and Friday immediately following the field trip.

For students involved in after-school sports, a shuttle bus will be available Monday afternoon to the High School , returning to Camp Pinnacle in time for dinner. On Tuesday, Students will return to the High School in time for sports team practices.

## Field Trip Schedule:

| | Monday 9/13 |
|---|---|
| 8:00 | Depart High School, front lot |
| 9-10:30 | Introductory meeting at Camp Pinnacle |
| 10:30-10:45 | Break |
| 10:45-11:45 | Curriculum workshop |
| 11:45-1:00 | Lunch |
| 1:00-3:00 | Low Ropes team building activity. Curriculum workshop (Students split into two groups) |
| 3:00-5:00 | Same activity, groups switch |
| 5:15-6:30 | Dinner |
| 6:30-7:15 | Team building workshop |
| 7:15-7:30 | Break |
| 7:30-8:30 | Team Building workshop |
| 9:00- 10:00 | Campfire |
| | Tuesday 9/14 |
| 8:00-9:00 | Breakfast |
| 9:00-10:00 | Team Building workshop (decision making skills) |
| 10:00-11:00 | Curriculum workshop (consensus training/Lab School rules) |
| 11:00-12:00 | Make tee-shirts |
| 12:00-1:00 | Lunch |
| 1:00-1:30 | Finish Consensus work |
| 1:30-2:00 | Wrap-up |
| 2:00 | Depart Camp Pinnacle |

Volume I, Issue 2                                        September, 1993

# FUTURES

Newsletter of the Bethlehem Laboratory High School, Delmar, NY  12054

## College Contacts Continue to Assist

by Judy Wooster

As we work to develop the Lab School program and assessment procedures, we are continuing to consult college admissions officers representing a variety of public and private colleges and universities favored by Bethlehem students. A recent round of calls solicited feedback on drafts of learning goals that will be expected of students in the Lab School. College admissions contacts describe the lists of learning goals as clear, specific, precise, detailed and useful.

With regard to the assessment approaches currently under development, college contacts suggest it will be important to have as much information as possible regarding student achievement on the learning goals. Those interviewed are enthusiastic about the multiple approaches proposed by the Lab School including portfolios, student self-evaluation, lists and narratives of personal and academic qualities, and records of performance on specific skills and content.

College admissions staff suggest some excellent ideas which will be considered by Lab School teachers in the coming months. We continue to find support and enthusiasm among our contacts for the innovative approaches that are the core of the Lab School Program.

Special thanks to Beverly Schwartz, Intern to the Assistant Superintendent, for her help in collecting these data. Please contact Judy Wooster if you have specific questions about the findings.

## REMINDER:

Lab School Overnight Field Trip to Camp Pinnacle, Monday, September 13 to Tuesday, September 14. Mail your parental permission slip and check for $55 (payable to *Bethlehem Central Schools*) TODAY to:

Michele Atallah
Bethlehem Lab School
700 Delaware Avenue
Delmar. NY  12054

## Read *This* First...

This issue of *FUTURES* brings several important items. One is the Lab School Progress Report (enclosed) that you will receive quarterly. The design of this document is intended to place the student's progress toward graduation front and center in a manner that is clear and concise. We have striven to present as much information as possible in as little space as possible while still keeping the report clearly understandable. We know you will let us know whether it works! Comments that reach us early in the semester will allow us to consider changes before the first report is out.

Second is the Lab School's Graduation Requirements (also enclosed). As the document itself states, the graduation requirements are a distillation of The New York State Regents Goals for Elementary, Middle , and Secondary School students, the guiding statement for curriculum development in New York State's public schools. Thus we stand on *terra firma* with respect to the legitimacy of our expectations for students.

Finally, you will find on this page and the next a number of articles on Lab School courses and college admissions matters. Again, please call the High School (439-4921) with your questions and comments, and leave a message for any of the Lab School teachers.

Enjoy the remaining weeks of summer vacation. We look forward eagerly to September!

– The Lab School Teachers

## THANK YOU...

...to Emrie LaBarge, computer professional and Lab School parent, who will be offering instruction to all Lab School students this fall on the fundamentals of *Clarisworks*, an integrated software program available on the Lab School's new computer.

...to Deneba Corporation for their generous donation of *Artwork*, a sophisticated painting and drawing program which we hope to put to good use this fall. (Thank you also to Emrie LaBarge for soliciting the donation on our behalf!)

# Science, Math Skills To Be Integrated

by Jane Feldmann

Our Lab School science/math program development is becoming more and more exciting as the summer progresses. Currently, we have established a valuable relationship with the Biology, Chemistry, and Physics Departments at Rensselaer Polytechnic Institute and have involved them in developing a challenging, integrated program of math and science that will prepare our graduates for the rigors of a college program. We will be continuing this dialogue as we move ahead and plan to establish a similar relationship with Siena College as well. In all of our work together, RPI faculty have been extremely supportive and excited about our directions.

You will see below the general outline of the science component for the course. Our math component is incorporating elements from Courses One, Two and Three that correspond to science topics. We are also establishing a relationship with the RPI Math Department. On September 22, our students will travel to RPI to visit the the Chemistry Department and speak with professors and researchers.

---

### General Outline of Lab School Science

Year One:    Physical and chemical components of
             our planet
Year Two:    Biological components of our planet
Year Three:  Science internship and senior
             interdisciplinary project

Note: Year's one and two may be reversed depending on student's year of graduation.

# Humanities Focus: language, literature, history

by James Nehring

The Lab School Humanities program will focus on Language, literature and history in a course that brings together elements of traditional English and social studies courses and more in an innovative unified program.

During the 1993-94 school year, the focus of the Humanities course will be American studies. In 1994-95, the course will focus on western studies. This two year sequence combined with coursework completed in ninth grade and in the senior year through the senior project and internship will set Lab School students well on their way toward meeting graduation requirements.

Some coursework will be prescribed and some elected by students who will complete course assignments and projects of their own design under teacher direction.

A trip to the New York State Farmer's Museum in Cooperstown is planned for the fall to study daily life in eighteenth and nineteenth century America.

---

# No one can do everything, but everyone can do something!

---

# Second Language Program To Stress *Joy Of Learning* !

by Michele Atallah

Bonjour! Hola! Marhaba! Oh what a wonderful feeling to be able to speak and to understand a second language. This is the Lab School goal for the second language program. We will concentrate on the communicative aspects of the language studied. The students will practice daily conversations using topics from either the language class or whenever possible the humanities or sciences classes. Integrating other curricula is a major difference between traditional school and the Lab school. Students will also read monthly magazines and clippings from newspapers that will

lead to discussions of cultural differences and similarities.

Computer software will reinforce vocabulary learning as well as writing. Students will also learn the slang used by their peers in different countries. The classroom will be conducted in the target language. Therefore every student will be required to buy a bilingual dictionary from the Buy It at the beginning of the year. There will not be as much emphasis on grammar and structure as in the traditional school, although proper usage will be explained and encouraged. This is the other major difference in philosophy.

Volume I, Issue 3                                        October, 1993

# FUTURES

Newsletter of the Bethlehem Laboratory High School, Delmar, NY   12054

## Overwhelming Response to Board of Examiners Invitation

An emphatic "Yes!" is the almost universal response to last month's letter of invitation to accomplished professionals around the region to serve on the Lab School's Board of Examiners.

Among those who will serve: New York State Assemblyman John Faso, New York State Senator Howard Nolan, General Electric Principal Technologist James Bennett, SUNY Binghamton Director of Admissions Geoffrey Gould, Senior Associate Dean of Admissions for Rensselaer Polytechnic Institute Jeanne Jenkins, Hudson Valley Community College Director of Admissions Linda Sweetman, Albany area businesswoman Laura Taylor, as well as several members of the Bethlehem Board of Education who bring a variety of expertise in government, academia, and business.

The Board of Examiners will join a panel of teachers to judge student written reports and oral presentations at twenty weeks and again at the end of the year. These reports and presentations, drawing on material studied in all core subjects will serve as mid-year and final exams for Lab School students.

The Board of Examiners will bring "real world" judgment to bear on our students learning and, we believe, make the evaluation of Lab School students considerably more authentic. We suspect also that the impressive level of accomplishment of our Board of Examiners will motivate students to do their absolute best work during mid-year and final exams.

## Back To School Night Reminder

On Thursday, October 21, The High School will host Back to School Night for parents. For Lab School parents, we encourage you to attend in order to meet the Lab School's Visiting Teachers. And, while the Lab School's Back to School Night was last month, we will offer a modified program in room 55 for part of the evening. Please listen for details when you arrive on the twenty first.

## Read *This* First

This issue of FUTURES brings you news of the first several weeks of school. We are off to a very good start. The overnight field trip to Camp Pinnacle was a great success. The team training and curriculum orientation that was conducted there laid a solid foundation for our work-- not to mention the many new friendships that were also established. The study skills workshops that we conducted later the same week have also paid off during the first few weeks of academic work as students become accustomed to the rigor of their courses. The recent field trip to Rensselaer Polytechnic Institute brought our students into direct contact with two emminent scientists in the fields of bio-chemistry and environmental studies. And during the weekly Community Meeting.students have been wrestling with the issues of justice and fairness as they craft the Student Judicial Council.

But there is always room for improvement and we are not satisfied with merely "good enough." Therefore, we have already undertaken some modest changes to address problems that have cropped up in the first few weeks. We were concerned that students were not getting enough class time for math during the sciences curriculum. Therefore we have added one period per week to the Sciences curriculum and re- apportioned periods so that math gets more attention as a discrete subject. We were also concerned that some students were growing frustrated that math was either too easy or too difficult. Therefore, on some days, students will be divided into two groups based on level of mastery in order to better meet the needs of all. Thanks to the insight and excellent planning of math teacher Sue Brockley, these changes have already been instituted.

We were concerned also that in group projects, students were sometimes hav ing to cover for a group member who was not doing his or her share. Most of the time students work well together, but occasionally someone does not.. While we wish to teach a sense of group responsibility, we do not want our student to have to bear the sole burden for seeing that classmates do their work. For that reason we have modified group projects in such a way that both team effort and individual

(Continued on page two.) .

Read *First...* (Continued from page one.)
effort will be closely examined.

We recently received a disturbing letter from Camp Pinnacle informing us of some property damage caused by our students. While the damage itself was not major ( a broken lamp, a torn pillow, three chairs left out in the rain, cigarette odor in some of the rooms), the fact that damage was done and that students were smoking in violation of our own rules as well as Camp Pinnacle's is disturbing. To their credit, several students have owned up to causing these problems and the terms of repayment are being settled. In addition, however, the entire Lab School is planning a follow-up field trip to Camp Pinnacle on Wednesday, October 27, to offer some community service. As we have stressed with students, this is not a punishment for all because of the deeds of a few. Instead, it is a statement that we as a school care what others think of us and that we believe our actions speak louder than our words.

Finally, with this issue of FUTURES you may find one or more Academic Progress Reports. We hope they are all good! But if they are not, we hope you will find them constructive and work with us to straighten out any academic problems.

So there you have it. As we said, we are very pleased with our progress so far but we are not content. Onward...

## A Word About Drug and Alcohol Abuse

As parents and teachers we are all concerned with potential substance abuse among teenagers. It is the policy of the Lab School to refer cases of suspected substance abuse to the High School's Core Team Program. For information about this program you may contact the High School. (439-4921). Furthermore, any student whom a Lab School teacher believes may be under the influence of a drug will immediately be referred to the High School administration.

## A Closing Thought

A Fact about geese: as each goose flaps its wings, it creates an "uplift" for the birds that follow. by flying in a "V" formation, the whole flock adds 71% greater flying range than if each bird flew alone.

Lesson: People who share a common direction and sense of commnity can get where they are going quicker and easier because they are traveling on the thrust of one another.

(From a speech, "Lessons From Geese," given by Angeles Arrien at the 1991 Organizational Development Network.)

# News From The Core Subjects

Sciences
Teachers: Sue Brockley, Jane Feldmann

In the math portion of sciences so far we have covered how to convert metric units and solve proportional problems. The problems have ranged from chemistry to everyday applications. We are moving toward the right angle and trigonometric ratios next, along with a review of scientific notation. Your children have had problem sets due on a weekly basis which are being used to evaluate their skill level along with tests and quizzes.

In the environmental chemistry portion of sciences we have been studying water quality, drawing on some of the recently learned math skills to look into methods of water filtration and how water behaves as a solvent with different substances. We are considering the implications of what we've studied for such real world applications as community water supplies. In addition, our work so far will be used as a tool to begin studying molecular structure.

Integrated Arts
Teacher: Michele Atallah

In Integrated Arts, students have moved away from the traditional lecture and drill format to an activity based program which has them hearing, speaking , writing, and in other ways practicing a second language for the full ninety minute block. To achieve this, the classroom has been divided into seven stations. Students spend fifteen minutes at each station completing an asignment and rotate through all stations in the course of the period. At one station, students listen to and watch native speakers on TV via satellite; at another station students use interactive software on the Lab School's computer. At other stations, there is practice in writing, culture, conversation, and more. Through the use of these stations, the teacher is free to move selectively from student to student and gorup to group addressing individual needs.

Humanities
Teacher: Jim Nehring

In Humanities, students are just completing a study of American life from the arrival of Columbus through the colonial period. We have read first hand accounts of a slave, an indentured servant, and early settlers, as well as known authors such as John Smith and poet Anne Bradstreet. Students have been writing in a variety of ways including fiction, essays, reviews and research.

Volume I, Issue 4                                    November, 1993

# FUTURES

Newsletter of the Bethlehem Laboratory High School, Delmar, NY 12054

## Highlights from Our First Ten Weeks

In addition to the Lab School's academic program, our first ten weeks have included much in the way of field trips and the development of some of the Lab School's distincitve features. Following is a summary

* Overnight Field Trip to Camp Pinnacle for Lab School Orientation.
* Field Trip to RPI for lectures and demonstrations by leading scientists in the fields of chemistry and environmental science.
* Establishment of the Student Judicial Council which has decided four cases to date.
* Return trip to Camp Pinnacle for community service. While there, we raked one truck load of leaves, moved two truck loads of split logs, cleaned the kitchen, filled holes, helped get out a major mailing, and painted two bathroom floors-- all in two hours!
* Field Trip to Capital Repertory Company's production of *Gang On The Roof.*
* Field trip to the Middle School for performance by Chestnut Brass Ensemble.
* Establishment of the weekly student advisory
* Numerous parent and student conferences

## How to Read Progress Report

The Progress Report enclosed with this issue of FUTURES is different from the usual high school style progress report. To help you navigate your way through, listed below is an explanation of symbols used in the Progress Report. Also, please note the narrative portion which you are to read, add to in the "Parent" space, and return to your child's teacher/advisor.
**Explanation of Symbols**
"S" indicates satisfactory progress toward graduation.
"U" indicates unsatisfactoy progress toward graduation.

6 indicates good work at the graduate school level
5 indicates godd work at the undergraduate college level
4 indicates good work for a high school senior
3 indicates good work for high school 10th or 11th grade
2 indicates good work for the 8th grade level
1 indicates good work for the sixth grade level

O indicates work not submitted that should have been
N/A (not applicable) indicates no substantial work in this goal area assigned/evaluated during the ten week period.

## READ *THIS* FIRST...

Lab School is hard work! That goes for students, for teachers *and* for parents. We appreciate the support parents have shown us in pushing our standards higher. And higher. You have been extremely responsive to our requests for help on the home front. The amount of time on the phone and in face to face conferences with you and your sons and daughters is certainly more than any of us have experienced previously. To say nothing of the untold hours at home with your child helping, cajoling, discussing, and encouraging. It is time consuming. It is hard work. And it will pay off.

The good news is that in various ways, students are beginning to rise to the challenge. For them, most espečially, the work is difficult. They have our support and our sympathy. All of our students are finding success in some ways; for some, a great deal, for others it will take more time.

The progress report enclosed with this issue of FUTURES most likely includes some "S"s and some "U"s. We hope that you and your son or daughter will interpret these as challenges met and challenges yet to be won. It is our fervent wish that no one views a "U" as failure! (See "What To Do About a "U", page 2.)

*Please return the narrative portion of the Progress Report with your (parent) comments filled in in the spaces provided.*

Whether your child has much or little to do to improve first quarter work, remember the pay off for all this work is substantial.. If we stay true to our standards, a Lab School diploma will become a mark of distinction for all who earn it. More than a mere certificate of attendance, it will certify a capable and mature individual.

Finally, please note the questionnaire enclosed with this mailing. We would appreicate your filling it out and returning it with the narrative portion of the progress report. The questionnaire relates to a variety of matters scattered throughout this issue of FUTURES.

## We Need Your Help

Many of you have offered generously to "help out in some way." We've found a way. Students are already beginning the process of signing up for their 1994-95 school program. We want to make sure that the Lab School is well represented so that all current ninth graders and their families who have an interest are aware and well informed of its features. We would appreciate your getting the word out in all ways possible. Tell your friends and neighbors! We are still small and relatively unknown. Also, there are some particular ways you can help us in this regard. Please see the enclosed questionnaire for details.

# Updates from the Core Subjects

## Sciences
by Sue Brockley and Jane Feldmann

We are continuing to look at the issues surrounding water. We are also beginning to look more seriously at the chemical structures in matter and will be looking closely at atomic structure. We are having an environmental soil and water specialist coming in to speak to the students about soil and water analysis.

Science and math are beginning to link together more now as we begin analyzing the percent concentration of solutions, the molar composition of compounds, and calculating the quantity of transfer in chemical equations. In addition, students are starting to study the concept of funciton in mathematics by first studying transformations and relating them to linear and quadratic functions.

## Humanities
by Jim Nehring

First, an explanation of humanities grades for the first quarter. Students scoring three or better in all sub-goals receive an "S" indicating satisfactory progress. Because first quarter topics are still under active study, there will be a number of opportunities to improve the scores. If, however, a student earned a score less than three in any sub-goal, he or she receives a "U" in humanities for the first quarter.

In class, students are exploring the period of early nationhood for the United States. We have read and analyzed the Declaration of Independence and are presently studying the Constitution. We will also be reading fictional works of the era by James Fenimore Cooper and Washington Irving.

On December 8, the entire Lab School will trek to Cooperstown where we will visit the Farmers' Museum, an outstanding, historical recreation of early 19th century American life. While there, students will participate in workshops recreating daily activities of the era.

## Integrated Arts (Second Language/ Second Culture)
by Michele Atallah

In Integrated Arts, we have been working on translations of children's books. During the week of November 15 to 19, students performed their translations-- recorded on ivdeotape- - in the Media Center. Once the taping is completed, students will edit their own work, and the best performance will be presented to elementary school students.

## Upcoming Events

Please mark your calendar now for a HOLIDAY PARTY to be held at Camp Pinnacle on Friday, December 17. The party will be open to all Lab School families, will include a meal, and, weather permitting, some fun outdoor activities. Details Re. transportation, cost, and time will be out shortly, so please hold that date.

Reminder: Field trip to Cooperstown on Wednesday, December 8. Permission slip and eleven dollars was due November 18.

## What To Do About A "U"

A "U" means unsatisfactory progress toward graduation in a particular area. If the "U" is in goal areas A through D, the best response is to strive to do better on work assigned during the second quarter. That's because goals A through D represent mostly *skills* for which there is continuous development. If the "U" is in a core subject under Goal E, then the student has until the end of the fifth week of the second quarter to take remedial action. Action should be taken right away since most items under Goal E represent *topics* which are covered for a limited amount of time. In some instances, remediation is built into the course; in others, it will require time after school as the teacher is available. Students should check with the appropriate teacher for details.

If an item in a core subject under Goal E is left unremediated after the fifth week of the second quarter, the next regularly scheduled opportunity for corrective action wil be in either the junior or senior year depending on the topic and course. We anticipate that most students will have *a few* such topics with scores below "4" as they enter their senior year. Therefore, part of the expected work of the senior year will be to "fill holes". Having too many unremediated topics, however, could delay graduation. That is not in itself a bad thing as the Lab School is dedicated to mastery . But it is nonetheless a reality that needs to be acknowledged. by the same token, more rapid mastery of goals and topics could lead to graduation sooner. This, too, is a real possibility.

## We Need Your Opinion Re. Feasibility of Big Spring Field Trip

The Lab School is considering an extended field trip to Toronto, Canada, from Thursday, May 19 to Saturday, May 21, 1994. A good estimate of the cost is $350, which includes the following: transportation by charter bus, hotel accomodations, some meals, ticket for *Phantom of the Opera* , The Science Museum, CN Tower tour, the Toronto Zoo, tour of downtown Toronto, stop at Niagara Falls on way back with Maid of the Mist boat ride, costs for chaperones, and a donation to support some scholarships for students whose families cannot cover the cost of the trip.

This trip would be a super way to begin winding up the school year, but we need to know if you think the cost is feasible. Please let us know by filling in and returning the enclosed questionnaire. Thank you.

## Please Remember To...

fill out and return the narrative portion of your child's progress report.

fill out and return the enclosed questionnaire.

Volume I, Issue 5 February, 1994

# FUTURES

Newsletter of the Bethlehem Laboratory High School, Delmar, NY 12054

## Lab School Students Stand and Deliver for Examiners

Imagine you've been asked to make a major presentation in connection with your work. You know a lot is riding on the presentation because your audience will include a state legislator, a leading research scientist from a major corporation, several university administrators, and numerous business managers from a variety of companies. Imagine, also, that your audience will have the opportunity to ask questions-- which means you've really got to know your stuff.

And imagine you're sixteen years old.

For three days during the final week of January, Lab School students were required to strut their stuff before a distinguished panel of examiners. Stressful? More than a little. Intimidating? You better believe it. Meaningful? Examiners commented that this is the kind of activity high school students should be required to do more often.

For the Lab School's twenty week exams, each student was required to write a major research paper, give an oral presentation of the paper, then answer questions extemporaneously about not their own paper, but the papers of their two partners.

Regardless of their scores, every Lab School student-- along with their parents-- should be proud of this accomplishment.

By the time a student graduates from the Lab School he or she will have made six major presentations before the Board. After that, college interviews will be a piece of cake. Oral presenttions during their college years and beyond will be the icing.

## READ *THIS* FIRST...

This issue of FUTURES brings you news of the Lab School's first-ever round of examinations before our Board of Examiners. You should be very proud of your son or daughter's accomplishment. Regardlessof his or her score, presenting before a distinguished panel is a significant achievement and a tremendous growing experience.

Also of note are the many individuals who have recently donated goods and services to the Lab School. They make the Lab School education richer and more meaningful for all our students, and we mention them below.

Please notice, also, on page two, that we are beginning to study a possible summer student contract program to remediate work from this school year. As we speak during the coming weeks, let us know what you think of the idea.

We have also re-worked the schedule as part of our on-going effort to "get the kinks out" of the Lab school program. We think you'll like the changes noted on page two..

## Lab School Students Helping Each Other With Time Management

With the change in schedule for the second semester. Math Teacher Sue Brockley is able to join the Lab School Advisory Program. Under her leadership we are launching a new (fourth) advisory group with a special mission: to assist students in better managing their time. On a voluntary basis students have joined this group to either offer or receive help in this area. We are so very pleased that a number of students have stepped forward to take part. We congratulate them for having the maturity to recognize their weaknesses and strengths.

## THANK YOU!

To Peter Staniels and the good people at Noreast Realty in Delmar for their generous donation of thirty office chairs. These good quality, welded, stackable chairs replace the aged folding chairs that our students have been using in Humanities and Second Language classes.

To the Saffady family of Delmar for their generous donation of a large screen color TV. Instead of sharing a TV among four classrooms, we now have one for every two classes for instructional use. Thank you also to the Bush family (Lab School tenth grader Joe) for letting the Saffady's know of our need.

## THANK YOU!

To Betty Wall of Delmar for her generous donation (on long term loan basis)of an IBM personal computer with internal modem.

To the numerous Lab School parents who recently served on a panel that met with parents of prospective students for next year.to offer impressions and answer questions. Thanks go to the Engelhardts, O'Neills, Corneils, McGraths, Martins, and Shortells. Thanks also to the many Lab School students who participated.

To Dennis Corrigan for putting us in touch with a number of persons and organizations that have already donated useful goods or whose donations are "in the works."

# Subject Area Updates

## Science, Math and Related Technologies
by Sue Brockley and Jane Feldmann

In environmental chemistry, students have just begun a unit of study focusing on non-renewable resources. They will examine the properties of elements and compounds on a global basis particularly as they relate to resource conservation.

In the math portion of the course there will be further development of the concept of functions and their application to everyday life. Projectiles will be studied, and for example, the trajectory of a golf ball. Later this semester, math students will begin a unit of study focusing on cryptology and the logic inherent in codes. Also, as we develop our computer lab, math students will begin programming in B.A.S.I.C. and Pascal.

## Second Language/ Second Culture
by Michele Atallah

With the new schedule, all classes are now single language classes. Now there's no excuse to speak English!

Our second Language program continues to emphasize practical language skills and fluency. Satellite TV programming in French and Spanish with follow-up discussions is an important part of the classroom experience. Also, we are looking into the development of a Hypercard stack on the Macintosh computer to enhance vocabulary lessons.

## Humanities
by James Nehring

In our most recent unit of study, students explored the history of the United States from the awakening of a national culture in the early 1800s to the era of Reconstruction after the Civil War. Along the way students read works by Poe, Emerson, Douglas, Stowe, Lincoln and others.

As a special project during this unit, students launched the Lab School's "Just One Computer" campaign in which each student wrote directly to the CEO of a Fortune 500 company or a locally based company asking for the donation of "just one computer" for a deserving, grass-roots, innovative high school program near Albany, New York. (Guess which one.) The assignment honed communication skills and provided a meaningful, real world opportunity for student work. It may also bring in some sorely needed technology.

Currently, students are studying the "Gilded Age." This week we are reading the work of W.E.B. Dubois and Booker T. Washington and studying their contrasting approaches to social change.

## Lab School Launches Improved Schedule Second Semester

In an effort to improve instruction, the Lab School has innaugurated a new schedule with the second semester. The new schedule offers the following improvements:
1) an additional period of math each week for all Lab School students;
2) reduction in class size from 27 students to 18 for most Humanities, Chemistry, and Second Language classes.
3) separation of all Spanish and French students into single language classes.

To achieve smaller classes without further increasing demands on teachers for instructional time, one period each week was taken from Advisory Group and Weekly Program. Our experience during the first semester suggests the new schedule will make for a more efficient use of time wihout compromising the quality of any of the Lab School's distinctive features.

Editorially, we would add it is *very nice*, because of the Lab School's small size, to be able to substantially reconfigure the schedule at will in order to improve learning– an option not possible in a larger program.

## Extemporaneous Speaking Skills

The Lab School will sponsor a mini-course focusing on extemporaneous speaking skills during weekly programs in February. The three session course will be led by Harold S. Williams, President of The Rensselaerville Institute and good friend of the Lab School. Like so many other gracious contributors to the Lab school's on-going work, Mr. Williams will be donating his services.

## Contract Program for Summer Remediation Under Study

The Lab School teachers are exploring the possibility of a summer remediation program that would involve Lab School students seeking to improve scores in self study and group study during the summer months. The contract program would culminate in written work to be submitted in September to be followed by exams to be administered during the first week of school. We would like to involve parents by having them verify study time. In order to take the September exam, a student would have to submit a time sheet signed by a parent. We will keep you posted.

## Lab School organizing Computer Lab

The Lab School is currently setting up a computer Lab with a cluster of four IBM computers which we expect to have in our possesion by the end of February. The Lab will be housed in the Math/Science Suite and will be available to students for all their computer needs. Ms. Brockley especially is thrilled at the improved opportunity that the computer lab will offer for programming instruction.

Volume I, Issue 6                                                                April, 1994

# FUTURES

Newsletter of the Bethlehem Central Laboratory High School, Delmar, NY   12054

## Lab School Parent/Teacher Workshop Slated

As follow-up to the Lab School's March 2 Breakfast, we will hold a parent/teacher workshop on **Tuesday, March 22, at 7 P.M.** in room 55-57 at the High School.

Please join us as we consider the questions identified under "Read This First" in the right hand column.

## Lab School Students Transforming Personal Interests Into Academic Projects

Matt Singerle will demonstrate his ability to think logically and creatively by planning and taking part in a winter camping experience. Betsey Languish will demonstrate her ability to set and achieve goals by training a three year old pony to drive in competition. Adam Prior will use reasoning skills to solve problems by designing a computer program to manage his summer lawn mowing business.

Lab School students have begun work this quarter on "portfolio projects." For this activity, each student identifies a personal interest in or out of school that he/she is currently not getting school credit for and shapes it into a project that demonstrates profieiency with one or more graduation goals.

The work, presently administered through the humanities course, requires each student to submit a proposal listing activities that will be undertaken, goals that the activities will apply to, and means of assessment. For some projects, adult verification is required. Students are urged to obtain consent form any adults they wish to involve in their projects erly in the process. Underway, progress is monitored by the teacher and some class time is provided for project work.

The range of possibilities is as wide as the experiences and interests of our students.

We encourage parents to help plan and develop the portfolio projects. Is there something that your daughter or son does which relates to a graduation goal? Keep it in mind for a future project and talk about it!

## Read This First...

"When I got that letter in the mail telling me my son might not graduate on time, I felt like I'd just gotten a final disconnect notice from the electric company." This comment, honest and heartfelt, was offered by a Lab School mother during a recent family/teacher conference. It is the same sentiment in different words that has been voiced by parents in a number of conferences we have recently held. And it raises some key issues that we must all attend to.

Our fledgling program faces a defining moment. It is vital that we all join our efforts to resolve in the best interests of your children-- our students--a number of questions:

1.   That students learn at different rates is so widely accepted it has become a truism. Yet society imposes the expectation on us that all students graduate at the same time (indeed on the very same day!), with their class. The importance of graduating "on time" is not trivial. It is tied into so much: the senior ball, commencement, the launching of a college career, summers back home with high school friends. And it stays with us throughout our lives through class reunions, and an abiding identification with "the class of __." The question is this: how do we address the desire to graduate "on time" *and* honor our commitment to a high school diploma that certifies a certain unquestionable degree of proficiency?

2.   The young people in this program are so wonderfully varied-- talented in different ways and needful in different ways. Each one deserves the utmost of attention from each teacher. At the same time, there are just four "permanent" teachers in this program (each of whom is required to teach high school courses as well), and while our staffing will increase significantly next year, so will the number of students. In short, the Lab School operates with the same student to teacher ratio as the High School. The demands on our teachers are great. Recently we have averaged three family conferences per week. In addition, we have tried hard to be available to our students after school. We have made every effort to offer opportunities for remediation. We work evenings, weekends and the early morning hours, reading assignments, constructing tests, planning lessons,

(Continued on Page 2)

## Read This First (continued from p. 1)

developing policies, all in the context of a brand new program where everything is done for the first time, and the community is looking on as we face our struggles and our triumphs. Conservatively, our teachers are working sixty hours each week. We are honestly approaching our physical and emotional limit. How do we balance the needs of our students against the time constraints of our teachers?

3. So many of our students work hard. We know they spend hours doing homework and many parents report to us that their child is working harder than ever before. The homework load for Lab School *is* demanding . Yet students, too, need down time. They need emotional space. How do we best help the children in Lab School to organize their time to balance their academic work with their lives?

These are three crucial questions. And we must face them together. You are a caring, committed group of parents. We are a dedicated, skilled group of teachers. Between us is a very talented group of young people. If we, in this little school of ours blessed with such favorable circumstances, can't crack this nut, then what public school anywhere can? Either we do it, or, realistically, it can't be done.

*Please join us on March 22!*

## Important Enclosures With This Mailing

This issue of FUTURES comes with a number of important enclosures. First please note the survey which the Bethlehem School District has developed as part of the Lab School's program evaluation. Please fill it out anonymously-- there is both a student portion and a parent portion-- place the completed forms in the envelope and return it to any of the Lab School teachers by March 25. It is very important in assessing our strengths and weaknesses that everyone fill out the survey. Your cooperation willbe greatly appreciated. Thank you!

Also enclosed is a mid-point progress report for the third quarter. You will notice that the Lab School has developed its own form here to replace the High School's customary blue forms. It is our desire to give you concise information relative to your daughter or son's progress. We hope you find the new method of reporting helpful.

Enclosed also, you will find an announcement for the Lab School's first-ever Pasta Dinner Fundraiser scheduled for Sunday April 10 from 5 to 7 P.M. We're looking forward to a fun and *profitable* time!

Finally, please note that the Lab School will host a Parent/Teacher workshop to follow-up the March 2 Breakfast.

## Lab School Students Learn Democracy Means Hard Work

"Democracy is the worst form of government except for all the rest." ·Winston Churchill's memorable comment on a system of shared power might describe our student's recent struggles and ultimate triumph in developing an important new policy for improving ·schoolwork.

Concerned about certain aspects of the Lab School's then-current policy for raising scores on school work, students brought the matter to Community Meeting on February 16. Next, a committee, assigned the task of revising the policy within certain guidelines set by the teachers, presented their proposal for a revised policy at the next Community Meeting. Two meetings and much long discussion later-- some of it quite steamy-- students and teachers adopted the new policy by consensus. (It appears below.)

We commend our students on several counts: 1) they hung in there to reach a decision that required a great deal of hard negotiating 2) On their own initiative, they have crafted an important new policy which in some respects demands more of them as students than the old. 3) Having taken part in the democratic process involving a matter of real consequence--not a simulation or game!-- they are now better equipped to assume their adult roles as citizens in a democratic society.

### New Assignment Policy

1. Lab School teachers will discuss due dates and stagger them as much as possible.
2. Work is expected to be turned in on time. Up to one week late, a student may turn in the assignment with the possibility of earning a maximum of 5-. From two to three weeks late, the highest grade will be a 4. After three weeks, the assignment may not be completed until summer (perhaps as a different activity in goal remediation).
3. Remediation policy: each paper a student gets back will have the date on it (the date it was handed back). The student has two weeks to remediate it and turn it back in. This two week system continues each time a paper is turned in-- however a real effort at the remediation process must be shown.
4. For the fourth quarter, the two week remediation period will be replaced with the exam period for papers handed during the last two weeks of classes.
5. The teacher reserves the right to waive the late penalty for extenuating circumstances.

## Desiderata...

A good school is sustained more by trust than by policies. Trust is nurtured through honest communication and pooled efforts.

*Volume I, ISSUE 7*

*May, 1994*

# FUTURES

Newsletter of the Bethlehem Laboratory High School, Delmar, NY 12054

## Lab School Parents/Students Raise $1800 with Pasta Dinner

With precise organization, coordinated teamwork, twenty gallons of tomato sauce and twelve hundred meatballs, Lab School parents and students served up 312 pasta dinners on Sunday April 10 in the BCHS cafeteria. Led by Darlene Dowse and Carol Berry, the small army of volunteers cooked, served, cleaned up, ran an auction of student services, and awarded door prizes resulting in a profit, after expenses, of $1800.

Anticipating perhaps two hundred customers-- though there was food for four hundred-- additional student waiters and waitresses were pressed into last minute service hastily setting tables and making way for the overflow crowd.

Door prizes included donations, rounded up by Pam Bolton-Engelhardt, from area merchants. In all, 50 door prizes were awarded. Student services auctioned at the event included yardwork, babysitting, catered meals, computer lessons, and ski repair for a total of twenty-two offerings.

Proceed from the dinner will go towards scholarships, field trips, awards and other important "extras."

---

### Pasta Dinner
### Special Thanks to...

| | |
|---|---|
| Darlene Dowse | Co-Chairperson |
| Carol Berry | Co-Chairperson |
| Nancy Martin | Room Set-up |
| Judy Languish | Salad,drinks,bread |
| Marilyn Corrigan | Purchasing |
| Pam Bolton-Engelhardt | Door prizes |
| Sheila DiMaggio | Publicity |
| Rus Kratz | Tickets |
| Pat Bush | Waiters/waitresses |
| Carolyn Wenger | Desserts |
| Bob James | Sauce/pasta prep. |
| Carole Doody | Clean up |

---

Note: Please return signed permission slip enclosed with this mailing for field trip to Ellis Island scheduled for Monday, May 9. Cost is $27. Departure time from High School front lot is 6:15 A.M. (Yikes!), returning @ 6:00 P.M. *(Let us know if you are in need of scholarship assistance. Funds are available!)*

## READ THIS FIRST...

This issue of FUTURES brings with it the third quarter report card (revised), along with news of the very successful pasta dinner and a remarkable gift from MCI Corporation. Also, please note we have included an overview of the 40 week exams with due dates. Also, subject updates on page two focus on upcoming topics of study. Ask your daughter/son how they're doing.

### Revised Progress Report With This Issue

As a result of two workshops with parents and teachers and numerous conversations with students, the Lab School begins use of a revised progress report with the third quarter.

The new progress report, enclosed with this mailing, looks similar to the previous version but includes one major change. Progress toward graduation goals A through D is now based strictly on portfolio projects. (Sample information on portfolio projects is enclosed.) Several smaller changes have also been made.

#### How To Read the New Progress Report

Goals A through D (page one): scores posted on this page represent work done in connection with portfolio projects. A portfolio project is a student designed project involving mostly out-of-classroom work intended to satisfy one or more graduation goals. Portfolio projects are extremely varied as they draw on the diverse personal interests of our students. Projects completed recently include, for example, a winter camping experience, a personally designed physical fitness program, photographic darkroom work, a traditional Native American vision quest, management of a lawn mowing business for forty two customers, a paper route, child care, and more.

Only those goals for which a project has been completed are marked with a score. That's why your child's report card probably shows only a handful of scores on page one. As more projects are completed, the report card will fill with scores. As goals are satisfied, students will need to direct their projects toward goals not yet addressed. Eventually, all goals, over a period of two to three years will be satisfied, moving a student toward completion of a major graduation requirement.

Goal E (page two and following): Scores on this page represent work done in connection with Lab School *(Please see p. 2, "Revised Progress Report")*

### Revised Progress Report (continued)

classes as well as mid-year and end-of-year exams. For each subject, topics dealt with during the current unit are listed together with the student's score. Similarly, mid-year and end-of-year exam scores are listed. In addition, this section of the progress report shows student progress with respect to a select number of academic skills employed in classroom (as opposed to project) work.

#### How Good Is Good Enough?

In order to earn a Lab School diploma, a student must earn a "4" in all graduation goals.For each goal area, however, that carries different implications. For goals A through D (page one), students will work continuously for three years on the same goals. Therefore earning "4's" right away is not essential-- as long as all goals have reached a "4" level by graduation.

For scores listed under subject areas on page two, it is more important that students earn "4s" with each report card. That is because the topics listed here are dealt with for only a limited amount of time before the class moves on. As a rule of thumb, a successful student should earn "4" or better on about three-fourths of the topics listed in this section. The remaining fourth could be raised through additional projects, possibly during the summer, or during the senior year.

For scores listed under "exams," a student should be showing "4s" consistently by the end of their junior year.

### Student Sarah Curtin Wins MCI Corporate Grant for Lab School

As the result of a letter composed by student Sarah Curtin, the Lab School has been invited by MCI Corporation to join their Community Outreach Program. Schools participating in this program are granted supplies, including computers, computer equipment, office furniture and more from MCI's warehouse of corporate "cast-offs." Participating schools pick items off MCI's inventory list. MCI pays all shipping charges and guarantees the equipment to be in good working order. And the offer is good on a continual basis. As schools have additional needs, they need only make further requests.

Sarah's letter, which highlighted the Lab School's unique features, caught the attention of MCI's Lee Allen, in charge of the Outreach program. Allen called the Lab School on April 8 from his office in McLean Virginia and introduced himself as "the guru of corporate giving for MCI." Naturally, we were all ears.

Sarah's letter was part of a Lab School letter writing campaign undertaken last fall in which each Lab School student wrote directly to the CEO of a Fortune 500 company requesting "just one computer" for the Lab School. Until April 8, students had received only "regrets" for their pleas.

Sometimes, persistence pays off. Congratulations, Sarah!

## Subject Area Updates
### *Major topics To Be Covered During The Fourth Quarter*

#### Math

Students will complete work on quadratic functions and begin a unit of study on cryptology to include work with number theory and computers. A revised math paper will be due during the fourth quarter.

Note: computer grade of "3" for the third quarter is acceptable for now since it represents work-in-progress. As the student progresses, it is expected that he or she will achieve a level of "4."

#### Humanities

During the fourth quarter students will be studying American history and literature since World War II. Major topics will include: 1) Truman and the Cold War; 2) Eisenhower and modern Republicanism; 3) Kennedy's New Frontier and Johnson's Great Society; 4) the Nixon years; and 5) the United States since 1974. Literature of each period will be studied in connection with the political and social history of the era.

The entire Lab School will take a day trip to Ellis Island and the Statue of Liberty on Monday, May 9, as a final outing for the American Studies course.

For those students taking the Advanced Placement Exam in U.S. History, the exam is scheduled for Wednesday, May 18. Students are completing several portfolio projects as additional preparation for the exam.

#### Second Language/Second Culture

Students studying French will take a major exam during the week of May 2 to 6. They will be resonsible fo r the following material: 1) Vocabulaire: S'appeler.....faible; 2) Lecture: La Baleine De Ker-Armor, read pp. 20-21, study vobabulary of the page; 3) Conversation: A l'ecole:study vocab.:Blairer-Frite; 4) Writing: Resumer:article 3; 5) Culture:Chapitre 3:read pp. 24-33; 6) Au magasin de chaussures:page 94.

Students studying Spanish will take a major exam during the week of May 2 to 6. They will be responsible for: 1) Vocabulary: La escuela... quedarle; 2) Reading: los cochinos, children's story; 3) article summary 1-3; 4) Conversation: at school,slang; 5) chapter 3, language, pp. 42-50; 6)computer: shopping for clothes, at the market, at the laundry.

Students undertaking independent should continue their work as assigned.

#### Science

Students will study the chemistry of petroleum and foods including viscosity of materials, chemical analysis of food groups, and effects of different organic chemicals on the body.

*Students should also be at work on their 40 week exam. See enclosed instruction sheet.*

Volume I, Issue 8　　　　　　　　　　　　　　May, 1994

# FUTURES

Newsletter of the Bethlehem Central Laboratory High School, Delmar, NY 12054

## Planning Continues for Lab School Transcript/ Senior Year

It must be attractive and readable. That's the advise from guidance counselors and college admissions offices consulted recently as the Lab School continues design work for its student transcript. A draft will be available by mid-summer, and, by September, the final version will be produced and ready for our first senior class as they begin the college application process.

For universities that process thousands of student applications, the transcript will be quickly understandable while still offering additional information beyond the first page for further evaluation of the student's high school work. For colleges more amenable to a "thick" transcript, the Lab School transcript will provide a rich representation of the student's abilities and accompliments.

As transcript design work goes on, so to the design of the Lab School senior year. The first semester of the senior year will consist of coursework in new material and material for remediation, development of a senior internship and research project, and completion of college applications (work on which will be conducted as part of the student's school program). The second semester will involved the execution of the internship designed during semester one and completion of the research paper.

## Lab School Students Tour Ellis Island, Statue Of Liberty

Over 100 million Americans can trace their family roots to an ancestor who passed through Ellis Island, and on May 10, Lab School students journeyed by bus and ferry to the immigrant processing center turned museum in new York Harbor. While there, students completed an assignment in which they assumred the role of an imaginary immigrant from a nation and era of their choosing and wrote a fictional letter home describing their arrival in America.

Highlights of the trip included the Wall Of Names where some students were able to identify grandparents and other relatives, exhibits of immigration history, a stunning view of Manhattan, a ferry ride to the Statue of Liberty, and, while standing at the base of the Statue, a near-total eclipse of the sun!

Thanks to Ms. Miner, Ms. Morrell, and Ms. Curtin, Lab School parents who served as chaperones. We commend our students, too, the vast majority of whom demonstrated maturity throughout the trip and gained a great deal from their experience.

## Read This First

This issue of FUTURES brings you an interim progress report, news of recent events, and important information on upcoming events. Please join us in commending your child for work marked "well done" in the progress report, and please support us in seeing that work marked "not turned in" or "needs to be finished/improved" is taken care of promptly. (A science update will be included on the next interim report.) Thank you!

## Upcoming Events

June 1-3: End-of-Year field trip to Silver Bay Camp on Lake George. Students will spend daytime hours in academic workshops and mini-courses. Late afternoons and evenings will be devoted to recreation and presentations. Workshops and mini-courses will be offered in SAT review (some of our students will take the SAT the day after they return), science topics, study skills, time management, history of the Adirondacks, and more. Evening Sessions will include a motivational key note speech by William Powell.

At night, a chaperone will be on duty in the student dormitories from late evening until breakfast, and students will be required to stay in their rooms.

Cost of this important field trip will be @ $120, including two nights lodging, three days of meals, and use of all facilities. Scholarship assistance is available. Please make your need known to a Lab School teacher and we will do our best to meet it in a discrete manner

May 25: Field trip to Capital Rep. theatre for a performance of *High Hat Hattie*, a true story of the first African-american to win an Academy Award. Your daughter/son should have already presented you with a parent consent form. Cost is $8, and scholarships are available.

June 14, 15, and 17: Lab School Final Exams. Each student will present and defend their second semester research paper together with a group of three of their classmates on one of the above dates. Presentations will take place between 8A.M. and 12 noon on all three days. Students should be present by 7:45 on the day of their exam and are required to stay and attend all presentations on that day.

We urge parents to attend as well. Please, please come and share in the work your child has done!

*(Continued on page 2.)*

## Upcoming Events
*(Continued from page 1.)*

May 21 to 26: Final Exam Rehearsals. Each final exam student group will be required to make a "dress rehearsal" presentation of their final exam before at least one parent. Please make arrangements with your child and parents of their group members. Each group must submit a signed "parent report" (on a form to be provided) by May 27. Sunday, June 19: End-of-Year Student Recognition Dinner. (Please see enclosure.)

## Please Note:
### Incident Results in Student Arrest and Suspension from School
While at Ellis Island for the May 10 field trip, three students were arrested by Ellis Island Rangers for possession of marijuana. Each student was cited and fined. Their parents were immediately notified and each student was suspended from school for five days. They will not be eligible to attend further field trips this year.

Drug use is a serious problem for our community and our schools. The Lab School takes a strong stand when our students are involved. We urge parents to join us in confronting the issues surrounding drug use in a firm and caring manner.

## Congratulations...
... Danielle Leonard for earning High Honors on the National French Exam and to Brian Corrigan, Amanda Crosier, and Betsey Languish for earning Honorable Mention.

... the following students who have taken on the challenge of the Advanced Placement Exam in U.S. History. We wish them well on the exam, May 18: Bryan Berry, Cailin Brennan, Megan Corneil, Sarah Curtin,, Celia Doherty, Jennifer Engelhardt, Liz Kadish, Emily Kratz, Betsey Languish, Danielle Leonard, Rebecca Matthews, Emily McGrath, Ben Miner, Tim Wenger.

## Slate of Examiners Finalized for June Exams
The Board of Examiners for Lab School exams, scheduled for June 14, 15, and 17 (See *Upcoming Events*, page one) will include the following persons: Harold Williams, President, the Rensselaerville Institute; Dennis Stevens, BC Board of Education; Cailin Brown, writer/reporter, *The Times Union;* Peter Trent, BC Board of Education; Lynn Lenhardt, BC Board of Education; Pamela Williams, Vice President, BC Board of Education Laura Taylor, President Laura Taylor, Ltd.; Gail Sundling, owner, Delmar, Bootery; Les Loomis, BC Superintendent of Schools; Gary Wenik, Chairman, Dept. of Chemistry, Rensselaer Polytechnic Institute.

## Parents Cadieux and Nixon Present at Weekly Program
Gaston Cadieux (Martin's father) and Suzanne Nixon (Ian's mother) presented during the Lab School's Weekly Program on May 4 and May 11 respectively.

In 1984, Gaston Cadieux flew to Nicaragua as a representative of *Witness for Peace* to observe nationwide elections. While there, he was moved by the plight of a pre-school in Managua that was struggling to serve some forty students with barely any materials. Today, he and his wife Noreen (who jointly operate Blossoms Montessori School here in town) serve a network of pre-schools in Nicaragua by providing assistance and training teachers. Mr. Cadieux's presentation, which focused on social justice issues, also involved students in a lively discussion of race and gender issues in our own school.

Suzanne Nixon, who holds a Ph.D. in history from the University of Wisconsin (Madison), spoke on the music and cultures of indigenous peoples from around the world. The presentation, which included authentic audio recordings, exposed students to ways of living and thinking dramatically different from their own while underscoring the essential humanity of all peoples.

A huge THANK YOU to Gus and Suzanne for sharing their time and talents with us! A belated thank you also to Mr. Morrell (Tina's father) who spoke to the Lab School last semester on issues surrounding water quality related to his work as an expert in gorund water quality.

What is *your* area of expertise? Call us, (We've already begun planning the fall schedule), and let's talk about how you could share your talents with our students. Don't be shy!

## Outside Interest in Lab School Grows
As word spreads of the hard work and innovations pioneered by Lab School students, teachers, and parents (as well as our growing pains!), the Lab School is attracting considerable outside attention.

On April 26, Ms. Atallah, Ms. Brockley, Ms. Feldmann, and Mr. Nehring jointly delivered the Keynote presentation for the Gideon Hawley Lecture Series at Union College attended by area educators. Ms. Feldmann was recently invited to serve on a State Education Department Committee exploring innnovation in science, math and technology, and Mr. Nehring has been invited to present at the annual convention of the National Council for the Social Studies.

Recent inquiries for materials or on-site visits have come from area schools/colleges including: Shenendehowa, Amsterdam, Ravena, Albany, Rhinebeck, Catskill, SUNY Albany, RPI, Siena, and Union.

We are in the process of establishing rules for on-site visits and guidelines for outside presentations in order to ensure that they do not interfere with the smooth running of our school.

Volume 1, Issue 9                                                    June, 1994

# FUTURES

Newsletter of The Bethlehem Laboratory High School, Delmar, NY   12054

## We Made It!

### *Lab School Completes First Year*

Hurray! We did it! Consider the following:

1. Every Lab School student studied a second language, science, and math, and will continue to throughout his or her high school program.

2. Every Lab School student has now presented twice before an imposing panel of experts (our Board of Examiners), and in almost every case experienced substantial improvement between the twenty week and forty week presentations.

3. Many Lab School students who struggled academically during the first semester have begun to prove to themselves and others that they CAN do it.

4. The strong bonds of friendship and mutual support evident at our end-of-the-year dinner are the result of just one year of our joined efforts.

5. In September we will be able to continue to grow as a community.

## College Update

We are in the process of obtaining feedback from college admissions offices regarding the Lab School transcript. We will continue to edit and revise over the course of the summer with the added help of BC's Guidance Department. Our plan is to have the final transcript ready and printed in quantity by September so that visiting college representatives--approximately two hundred of whom come through the High School during the fall-- will each receive one as part of a Lab School "press kit," and Lab School students will be able to send them to colleges of interest to them.

### Wojcik Joins Lab School Faculty

On Wednesday, June 15, The BC Board of Education approved the appointment of William Wojcik to a full time English position in the High School including a partial assignment to the Lab School. Mr. Wojcik, who has taught at the High School for one year already, holds a master's degree from Union College and Bachelor's degree with a major in English from SUNY at New Paltz.

Mr. Wojcik will join Mr. Nehring in teaching the humanities curriculum to Lab School tenth and eleventh graders. With decided expertise in the teaching of writing and literature, as well as enthusiasm for his Lab School assignment, Mr. Wojcik brings a wealth of new learning opportunities for our students. We are thrilled to welcome him aboard.

## Read This First:

This issue of FUTURES brings you the fourth quarter report card along with information regarding summer remediation, end of the year activities, and upcoming September events.

We are proud of what our students have accomplished in their first year of Lab School. It hasn't been easy for them. The growth we have observed in academics and personal maturity has been tremendous. We are excited to know that next year we will be able to continue working with these same students and take them still further in their development.

## Students Inititate Summer Portfolio Projects and Remediation Plans

Together with their teachers, Lab School students have developed plans for the summer months that may include portfolio projects, and/or remediation of topics from the 93-94 school year. Work on portfolio projects is entirely optional and results mainly from students wishing to earn credit for an already planned summer activity (an excellent idea which we whole-heartedly support!).

As previously announced, remediation of topics from the 93-94 school year has been urged for any student who scored less than "4" in 25% or more of their subject area topics. We hope you have been in communication with your son or daughter about their summer work plans. All work is due on the first day back to school (Thursday, September 8)

## Mark Your Calendar Now: *September Parent/Teacher Gathering*

7:30 P.M., Friday, September 9, 1994, at the home of Michele Atallah, 645 Morris Street, Albany. Details to follow. Organizer: Mary Miner (439-2941)

## THANK YOU!

The Lab School teachers wish to thank the many parents for their expressions of support throughout the year. Your letters, cards, and phone calls often arrived at just the right moment and have meant a great deal. Thank you!

## Lab School Students Earn Awards for Academic Excellence

On June 19, at the end-of-the-year Awards Dinner, students were honored for achievement, improvement, and effort according to the Lab School's five graduation goals. A complete list of award recipients follows:

**Adept thinker and problem solver:** Brian Corrigan, Betsey Languish

**Capable and committed citizen:** Megan Corneil, Brandon Macomber

**Able communicator:** Bryan Berry, Amanda Crosier, Jeffrey Wellman

**Confident and mature individual:** Cailin Brennan, Danielle Leonard, Ian Nixon

**Scholarship in science:** (excellence)Celia Doherty, Elizabeth Kadish, Betsey Languish (effort/improvement) Cailin Brennan, Theresa Cleary, Brian Corrigan, Christopher Lang, Danielle Leonard, Emily McGrath

**Scholarship in math:** (excellence) Celia Doherty, Elizabeth Kadish, Betsey Languish (effort/improvement) Bryan Berry, Cailin Brennan, Amy Dowse, Brandon Macomber, Kiley Shortell, Timothy Wenger

**Scholarship in Second Language/Second Culture:** (excellence in Spanish) Elizabeth Kadish (excellence in French) Cailin Brennan, Celia Doherty, Danielle Leonard (effort/improvement in Spanish) William Sanchez-Silverman, Amy Schron, Kiley Shortell (effort/improvement in French) Brian Corrigan, Amanda Crosier, Betsey Languish

**Scholarship in Humanities** (excellence) Elizabeth Kadish, Emily McGrath (effort/improvement) Bryan Berry, Cailin Brennan, Brian Corrigan, Amanda Crosier, Danielle Leonard, David Martin, Ian Nixon

### Please Note:

As the result of a meeting with the Lab School Impact Committee at the High School, the Lab School faculty has agreed that future Lab School fund raisers will be used solely as a community service project, which will contribute money for field trip scholarships and donations to charitable organizations. No money will be used to supplement curriculum or program.

### A Thought:
*Some people say time changes things.*
*Actually, you have to change them yourself.*
*--Andy Warhol*

## Seniors:
### *Where Do You Want to Go?*

Summer is the ideal time to visit colleges, and we encourage all our students, but particularly seniors, to visit colleges they are considering applying to. Many excellent colleges lie within several hours drive and offer an ideal opportunity for a summertime day trip. Go with friends, or make it a family outing. *And bring back materials to share!*

## A Poem:
### Lab School, First Year

We began with 54, plus the teachers, that's four more.
We had teams, there were two, one green, the other blue.
Up to Camp Pinnacle we went, the girls in a hotel, the guys in a tent.
We were creatures of the night, and, yes, we paid for it in the light.
A lamp and some chairs we did break. But we said we were sorry with paint brushes and a rake.
Around the campfire we told some deep stuff, for some it was easy for others rough.
Our sad attempts at making a theme song helped us laugh the days along.
We had a good time and we all wanted to stay, but little did we know we would have Silver Bay.
The work at first seemed like a breeze, but when class kicked in it wasn't done with such ease.
Mrs. Brockley complained that there wasn't enough Math; poor Mr. Nehring had to face here wrath.
Some chemistry student left stuff in the sink; in community meeting Mrs. Feldmann made a stink.
Mrs. Atallah was always enthusiastic, which made Monday morning classes absolutely fantastic.
During his lectures the students sat peering and wondering, "Why you gotta where those shoes, Mr. Nay Ring?"
The teachers went to conventions, leaving us astray. Mr. Jones and Mrs. Robinson got to teach for the day.
The memories were many, sledding, Cooperstown, Capital Rep.
These were learning experiences, to say the least, but the most profitable, our spaghetti feast.
I wrote this poem instead of a skit because no matter how hard we try, we can't imitate you a bit.
We've had many teachers before, but none have come close to these four.
I'm sure at times we were all a pain, but our respect and friendship you did gain.
High School here lasts three years, maybe two. Not to be mean, but after that, I hope we don't see you.
Congrats to the senior Lab Rats and good luck. When you're rich and famous, send us a buck.
I'll see the rest of you in September, but the first year of Lab School I'll always remember.
I can't believe the year is over, but hey, Mr. Nehring, next year, how about Grover?
– Dan Mawhinney, Kiley Shortell